Searching for Excellence & Diversity

SEARCHING FOR

EXCELLENCE

&

DIVERSITY

A GUIDE FOR SEARCH COMMITTEES
National Edition

"We need diversity in discipline, intellectual outlook, cognitive style, and personality to offer students the breadth of ideas that constitutes a dynamic intellectual community."

WISELI
Women in Science & Engineering Leadership Institute
University of Wisconsin-Madison

Eve Fine and Jo Handelsman

TABLE OF CONTENTS

ACKNOWLEDGEMENTS

This book would not have been possible without the support we received from our colleagues at WISELI: Molly Carnes, Jennifer Sheridan, and Julia Savoy. Their willingness to review, edit, and proofread multiple drafts of this document is greatly appreciated and their suggestions have strengthened and improved this text. We also thank Luis Piñero and Elizabeth Bolt for reviewing this edition and for their valuable contributions to our workshops for search committee members at the University of Wisconsin-Madison.

This guidebook incorporates information, experiences, questions and concerns shared with us by the many faculty and staff at UW-Madison and at universities and colleges across the nation who have participated in our workshops for search committees. We thank them for their participation and hope that this guidebook proves useful in their ongoing efforts to recruit and hire new faculty members.

We also wish to thank individuals who contributed to the first edition of this guidebook: Molly Carnes, Bernice Durand, Randy Durand, Rosa Garner, Linda Greene, Steve Lund, Luis Piñero, Christine Pribbenow, Dean Pribbenow, Jennifer Sheridan, and Hilary Handelsman; and to acknowledge the contributions of the following University of Wisconsin–Madison faculty members who helped test initial drafts of this material in pilot workshops: Donna Fernandez, Aaron Friedman, Guri Sohi, Jim Steele, Mariamne Whatley, and Brian Yandell. Finally, we thank the following WISELI staff for their help with the original guidebook and initial workshops: Deveny Benting, Sarah Marxhausen, and Jessica Winchell.

Preparation of this guidebook was made possible by grants from the National Science Foundation (NSF #0123666 and #0619979). Any opinions, findings, and conclusions or recommendations expressed in this material are those of the author(s) and do not necessarily reflect the views of the National Science Foundation.

IMPORTANT NOTES

This guidebook is intended to supplement, not to replace, any official search handbooks that may govern the search process at your institution.

All search committee chairs and members should be thoroughly familiar with the policies and procedures outlined in any official documents developed by your institution.

This guidebook provides advice from experienced and successful search committee chairs and from research and advice literature on academic search strategies.

It is expected that you will modify, adjust, and/or adapt these recommendations in accordance with such factors as the size of your search committee and pool of candidates, the breadth of areas encompassed in the position description, and the standards of your discipline.

INTRODUCTION

Hiring and retaining an excellent and diverse faculty is a top priority for colleges and universities nationwide. Vast amounts of time and considerable monetary resources are devoted to searching for and hiring new faculty. If the search is successful and results in the hiring of productive faculty who make valuable and lasting contributions to the discipline and the university, the time and money are well spent. If the search is unsuccessful or newly hired faculty do not remain in their positions, the time, effort, and expenses incurred in conducting repeated searches can become burdensome. Consequently, many universities are looking critically at their hiring processes and are recognizing that faculty search committees receive little education about the process. These schools are implementing programs to provide faculty with information, advice, and techniques that will help them attract excellent and diverse applicant pools, conduct fair and equitable evaluations, and successfully hire new faculty members who will contribute to the excellence and diversity of their institutions.

This guidebook serves as a useful resource for schools, colleges, and/or universities seeking to implement educational programs for faculty search committees. It can also serve as a resource for individual members of a search committee.

The guidebook consists of six sections—Six Essential Elements—each targeted at a specific stage of the search process.

- Element I, "Run an Effective and Efficient Search Committee," focuses on the earliest stages of the search process—before the committee has begun recruiting applicants. It provides advice and suggestions for building an active and involved search committee and for establishing policies and practices that will help increase the effectiveness of the search.

- Element II, "Actively Recruit an Excellent and Diverse Pool of Applicants," recommends that search committees engage in discussions of both diversity and excellence before writing position descriptions or announcements, developing evaluation criteria, and recruiting applicants. It provides suggestions for initiating such discussions. This section recommends that search committees take an active approach to recruiting and provides suggestions and resources for doing so.

- Element III, "Raise Awareness of Unconscious Assumptions and their Influence on Evaluation of Applicants," presents research findings from a variety of disciplines (including cognitive psychology, social psychology, economics, and organizational behavior) that demonstrate how unconscious assumptions can influence the evaluation of applicants.

- Element IV, "Ensure a Fair and Thorough Review of Applicants," relies on research findings to suggest methods for overcoming the influence of unconscious bias and assumptions on the evaluation of applicants. It also provides suggestions and instruments for conducting equitable evaluations.

- Element V, "Develop and Implement an Effective Interview Process," provides advice and recommendations for conducting interviews and on-campus visits. This section stresses the importance of recognizing that interviews and on-campus visits not only provide search committee and departmental members with the opportunity to evaluate candidates, but also provide candidates with opportunities to evaluate their potential colleagues, the department, the college or university, and the community. This section presents advice for utilizing principles of "universal design" to conduct interviews and on-campus visits that meet the needs of candidates with and without disabilities. It recommends designing a campus visit that will be a good experience for all candidates—whether or not they are the candidate hired.

- Element VI, "Close the Deal: Successfully Hire your Selected Candidate," provides advice and suggestions for encouraging your selected candidate to accept your job offer.

Each of these six sections aims to help search committees improve the effectiveness and efficiency of all activities related to recruiting and hiring new faculty members. By following the recommendations outlined in this guidebook, search committees can expect to attract applicants who not only meet or exceed expectations in terms of qualifications, but also reflect the diversity present in the potential applicant pool. The advice and recommendations in the guidebook aim to help search committees improve their chances of hiring faculty who will contribute to the excellence and diversity of their institution.

The definition of "excellence" will necessarily vary by institution, department, and even position. This guidebook encourages search committees to think carefully and strategically about what is "excellent" or "best" for each position given the needs and resources of their department, school, college, or university at a particular point in time. It recommends that search committees rely on their developed definition/s of excellence to inform their advertisements or announcements, efforts to recruit applicants, and criteria for evaluation.

The definition of "diversity" may also vary. Consequently, this guidebook encourages search committee to discuss what "diversity" means to them individually, what "diversity" means for their department, and why it is important for the department to strive to increase faculty diversity. In general, this guidebook encourages search committees to develop very broad definitions of diversity. Our nation's universities and colleges need diversity in discipline, intellectual outlook, cognitive style, and personality to develop a dynamic intellectual community. Diversity of experience, age, class, physical ability, religion, race, ethnicity, gender, and sexual orientation are just some of the qualities that contribute to the richness of the environment for teaching and research.

In discussing diversity, search committee members should examine their own departments and consider the extent to which they do or do not reflect the diversity they desire. Because women are underrepresented in many disciplines (especially in science, technology, engineering, mathematics, and academic medicine) and specific minority groups are underrepresented in most disciplines, this guidebook offers suggestions and advice for recruiting and ensuring fair evaluation of women and members of underrepresented minority groups. The term "underrepresented," in this context, means that a particular group's proportionate representation in the academy, or in a field of study, is smaller than its representation in the population at large.

It is important to recognize that considerable diversity exists within the categories "women" and "underrepresented minority groups." "Women" includes not only white, heterosexual women but also women of color, of different sexual orientations, physical abilities, religions, ethnicities, and more. Members of "underrepresented minority groups" include men and women with varying sexual orientations, physical abilities, religions, and ethnicities, who are also of African American, Hispanic, Native American, Native Hawaiian, and Native Alaskan descent. In some areas of the country, other minority groups, such as the Hmong, may be underrepresented. In some academic disciplines, additional minority groups may be underrepresented. For example, Asian Americans are not underrepresented in the academy in general, but may be underrepresented in leadership positions and within some fields in the social sciences and humanities.

While this guidebook concentrates on advice and resources for recruiting and evaluating underrepresented groups, search committee members can and should extrapolate from this advice to ensure that their recruitment efforts and evaluation processes will help them achieve the breadth of diversity they desire in their applicants. For example, schools or departments that are and have historically been female dominated, such as social work or nursing, can adapt the advice provided to ensure that they reach male candidates and avoid bias in the evaluation and interviewing processes. Similarly, departments seeking to be more inclusive of persons with disabilities, to expand research and enrich curricular content surrounding disability studies, and/or develop assistive technologies can adapt these recommendations for active recruiting to ensure that they are reaching individuals who study and/or have disabilities. In addition, they can use other portions of the guidebook to avoid biases and barriers in their evaluation and interview processes.

Each department's efforts to diversify its faculty in ways that are relevant to the department, its students, and the discipline will not only enrich the scholarly work of the department and the educational experience of its students, but will also contribute to the establishment of universities and colleges that reflect the students and communities they serve.

Essential Elements
of a
Successful Search

I. RUN AN EFFECTIVE AND EFFICIENT SEARCH COMMITTEE

Preparation: Before the search committee meets (pp. 6–7)

Tips and guidelines: Running an effective and efficient search committee (pp. 7–13)

Preparation: Before the Search Committee Meets

1. **Build a diverse search committee**
   A committee composed of diverse members can benefit from the variety of perspectives and new ideas each member provides. Think broadly and creatively about building a diverse committee. Including women and members of underrepresented minority groups on the search committee is highly recommend as a means of increasing the diversity of committee membership—but should not be regarded as the only means of doing so. Some search committees also increase diversity by including graduate students, members of the department's research staff, faculty members from external but related departments, and/or professionals working in related industries. This approach can help departments balance decisions about including women and/or minority faculty members on search committees with efforts to ensure that they are not overburdening individuals from underrepresented groups with service obligations.

   The perspectives and experiences of diverse committee members can enhance efforts to recruit applicants and evaluate candidates. Beware, however, of relying upon women and/or minority members of your search committee to be the only advocates for diversity. This can create a climate within the search committee and the department that will hamper your efforts to recruit and hire excellent and diverse candidates. Every member of the committee needs to be responsible for recruiting diverse and excellent applicants and for conducting fair and equitable evaluations.

2. **Schedule your first meeting well before your application deadline**
   Hold your first meeting well before your application deadline. This will allow the committee to develop and implement an effective recruitment plan and will provide the time needed to discuss and establish criteria for evaluating applicants.

3. **Know about and adhere to institutional policies and procedures and federal and state laws that govern the search process on your campus**
   Many universities and colleges publish documents (either print or web-based) that explain policies and procedures governing faculty searches, offer guidelines for search committees, and provide forms that require completion. Determine whether your campus produces such documents and, if so, become familiar with these documents, the advice they provide, and the requirements you need to follow. Doing so very early in your search process can save considerable time and frustration.

   State-supported universities and colleges may be subject to state laws that apply to search committee proceedings. In addition to state-specific laws regarding equal opportunity and affirmative action, these laws may also pertain to record keeping for the search and may stipulate requirements for whether and when to hold open or closed search committee meetings. If your campus does not publish guidelines that include discussion of the applicability of state laws to your search, consult with an appropriate colleague in your office of legal affairs, human resources, or equal opportunity and affirmative action.

   All universities and colleges (state-funded and private) are subject to federal laws governing equal opportunity. In addition, all institutions that accept federal funding for educational or research purposes are subject to affirmative action laws.

   - **Federal Equal Opportunity Laws** prohibit employment discrimination based on race, color, religion, sex, national origin, disability, or age. (State laws, as indicated above, may prevent discrimination against additional categories, e.g., sexual orientation, marital status, conviction record, and more.) For more information see: www.eeoc.gov/eeoc.

- **Federal Affirmative Action Laws** require institutions that receive federal funds to develop and implement plans "to recruit and advance qualified minorities, women, persons with disabilities and covered veterans." These plans should be incorporated into written personnel policies, kept on file, and updated annually. For more information see: www.dol.gov/dol/topic/hiring/affirmativeact.htm.

Rely upon your institution's policies and procedures and applicable state and federal laws as effective tools to help you maintain the integrity of your search process.

Tips and Guidelines: Running an Effective and Efficient Search Committee

Building rapport among committee members

1. **Gain the support of committee members**
   In productive search committees, the committee members feel that their work is important, that each of them has an essential role in the process, and that their involvement in the search process will make a difference. To generate such perspectives, the chair and each committee member can set the tone in the first meeting and can try to make sure that every member of the committee feels involved, valued, and motivated to play a significant role in the search. Some tips include:

   - Begin with brief introductions to get committee members talking and comfortable with each other. Do not assume that members already know one another—this assumption may not be correct, particularly if the search committee includes a student representative or members from outside the department. Provide and use name tags until you are confident that **all** committee members know each other.

   - Be enthusiastic about the position, potential applicant pool, and composition of the search committee.

   - Remember that in this age of tight budgets each position is precious and that it is up to the committee to ensure that the best candidate is in the pool.

   - Understand that the search process is far more idiosyncratic and creative than the screening process—each committee member can put his or her individual stamp on the process by shaping the pool.

   - Appreciate each committee member for the critical role he or she is playing by helping to select future faculty who will represent the department and the university for years to come.

2. **Actively involve all committee members in discussions and search procedures**
   Active involvement of every member of the committee will contribute to a more effective search. Such involvement will help the committee reach a broader base of applicants and conduct more thorough evaluations. To generate active participation, implement the following suggestions:

   - Look at each member of the committee while you are speaking.

- In the first committee meeting, engage in at least one exercise in which every committee member participates. This might be a discussion of the essential characteristics of a successful candidate or a brainstorming session about people to contact to help identify candidates.

- Try to note body language or speech habits that indicate someone is trying unsuccessfully to speak and then give them an opening.

- Be especially sensitive to interpersonal dynamics that prevent members from being full participants in the process. Many of us may assume, for example, that senior faculty are more likely than junior faculty to have connections or ideas about people to contact for nominations, or that students will be less critical in their evaluations. Sometimes these assumptions are correct, but we have all had our assumptions challenged by the junior colleague who nominates a great candidate or the student who designs an insightful interview question.

- Before leaving a topic, ask if there are any more comments, or specifically ask members of the committee who have not spoken if they agree with the conclusions or have anything to add. Be sure to do this in a way that implies you are asking because the committee values their opinion; try not to embarrass them or suggest that they need your help in being heard.

3. Run efficient meetings

The first meeting can be a lot like the first class of a semester or the first day of rounds—it shapes committee members' attitudes about the process and their role in it. Strive to help committee members recognize that attending committee meetings and the committee work they do outside the meetings is a good use of their time and that their participation will make a difference. Some tips to achieve this include:

- Rely on an agenda with time allotted to each topic and generally try to adhere to the plan.

- Begin meetings by reviewing the agenda and obtaining agreement on agenda items. If one committee member is digressing or dominating a discussion, gently and politely try to redirect the discussion by referring back to the agenda (e.g., "If we are going to get to all of our agenda items today, we probably need to move to the next topic now").

- If you deviate from the agenda or run over time, acknowledge this and provide a reason (e.g., "I know we spent more time on this topic than we had planned, but I thought the discussion was important and didn't want to cut it off"). Doing so will help committee members feel their time was well spent, that the meeting was not a random process, and that they can anticipate useful and well-run meetings in the future.

- Try to end meetings on time so that all committee members are present for the entire discussion.

Additional advice on How to Lead Effective Meetings is available from the University of Wisconsin–Madison (UW–Madison) Office of Quality Improvement and Office of Human Resource Development: http://go.wisc.edu/77c0c6.

Tasks to accomplish in initial meetings

1. Discuss and develop goals for the search

Engage in a discussion of goals for the search and use the agreed upon goals to develop recruitment strategies and criteria for evaluating applicants.

2. Discuss and establish ground rules for the committee

Establishing ground rules for the committee at the outset can set expectations, maximize efficiency, and prevent conflicts from arising later. Ground rules should cover such items as:

- **Attendance**

  The work of a search committee is cumulative and it can be very frustrating when a member who has missed one or more meetings raises issues and/or questions already discussed at previous meetings. More importantly, evaluation of applicants can be compromised if one or more committee members are not present for the discussion of all applicants' qualifications. Establishing policies regarding attendance and participation of search committee members can help avoid these complications. Some committees require all search members to attend all search committee meetings and activities and stipulate that members who do not attend must accept decisions made while they were absent. Other committees recognize that complicated schedules can prevent members from attending all meetings and establish policies permitting absent members to reopen discussions of issues considered at meetings they missed. Establishing such policies in advance will clarify expectations and reduce frustrations. Committee chairs can also help prevent absences by scheduling meetings well in advance. If possible, establish a schedule of meetings at the outset.

- **Decision-making**

  How will the committee make decisions? By consensus? By voting? It is important to determine this at the outset. Each method has its strengths and limitations. Voting is quickest, but a simple majority does not always lead to effective implementation of or satisfaction with decisions. Consensus may take longer to reach, but can lead to greater support for and comfort with decisions.

- **Confidentiality and disclosure**

  "One of the biggest challenges of maintaining confidentiality within the search is avoiding off-the-cuff informal comments search committee members may make to colleagues," says John Dowling, Sr. University Legal Counsel, UW–Madison. He recommends keeping the process as focused and self-contained as possible and advises search committee members to avoid discussing the specifics of the search with anyone outside the search committee until finalists are announced. Most institutions agree that, at a minimum, search committee members should keep deliberations about the merits of individual applicants strictly confidential. Such policies not only respect and protect the privacy of applicants, but also that of the committee or hiring group. "Those making the selection must be free to discuss applicants during committee meetings without fearing that their comments will be shared outside the deliberations. The names of candidates who have requested confidentiality should not be mentioned even in casual conversations. This information should be held confidential in perpetuity, not just until the search is over."[1]

  While it is important to maintain confidentiality about search committee deliberations, it is equally important to share general information about the search with the larger department, especially if the department will later play a role in evaluating candidates. The search committee should make reports to the department that provide information about

---

1. University of Wisconsin-Madison, Office of Quality Improvement and Office of Human Resource Development, "Academic Leadership Support: Confidentiality," http://go.wisc.edu/3idbel, accessed 9/11/2012.

the stage of the search; recruitment strategies; the quality and general demographics of the applicant pool; the policies the search committee is relying on to conduct fair and equitable evaluations; the selection of finalists; and more.

Some search committees and departments choose to make applicants' materials available for review by departmental members who are not serving on the search committee and to solicit input from these reviewers. In such departments, it is important to ensure that each individual who examines applicants' materials is aware of his or her obligation to maintain the applicants' confidentiality, and that discussions and deliberations about applicants' merits are confined to committee meetings in which the commitment to confidentiality is clear. Search committees and departments that follow this procedure should also:

- o Strive to make sure that all departmental members have equal opportunities to provide feedback.

- o Be aware of the possibility that candidates known to departmental members may be advantaged or disadvantaged in comparison to candidates not known to departmental members.

- o Account for the possibility that women or minority candidates underrepresented in their field may be less likely to be known by departmental members.

Efforts to balance requirements of confidentiality for applicants with openness about the search process can foster involvement and support from departmental members. Departmental knowledge about the progress of the search can also serve to hold a search committee accountable for recruiting and fairly evaluating a diverse applicant pool that includes women and members of underrepresented minority groups.

- **Other common ground rules**
  The committee may wish to establish other common ground rules including turning off cell phones, routing pagers to an assistant, being on time, giving all members opportunities to speak, and treating other committee members with respect even if there is a disagreement. Whatever ground rules the committee establishes should represent a consensus of the entire committee. They may need to be reviewed and updated periodically.

3. **Discuss roles and expectations of the search committee members**
   Committee members should know what is expected of them in terms of attending meetings, building the applicant pool, and evaluating applicants. **Committee members should also recognize that participation in a search will require considerable time and effort.** Some of the roles or expectations for search committee members include helping to:

- publicize the search
- recruit applicants
- develop evaluation criteria
- evaluate applicants
- develop interview questions
- interview candidates
- host candidates who interview on campus
- ensure that the search process is fair and equitable
- maintain confidentiality

It is important for committee members to understand precisely what role they will play in the selection of candidates. Will they be making the selection of finalists, ranking finalists for the department chair, or recommending finalists to the department or department chair? Will they select the candidate who receives a job offer? Or, will the department, the department chair, or the school or college's dean make the selection? There is wide variation—both across and within schools and colleges—in the roles search committees play in this process. Search committee members who discover late in the process that their role is not what they had originally expected may experience great frustration or believe that their time was not well spent.

4. **Review institutional policies and procedures for search committees**

5. **Raise and discuss issues of diversity**
Use the material on pp. 16–19 and pp. 36–41 to guide your discussion.

6. **Discuss what "excellence" means for the position you are seeking to fill**
Begin to discuss and build consensus about the qualities and qualifications needed for this position and about the relative weight of each criteria. In conducting this conversation, keep in mind the needs and desires not only of the individual members of the committee, but also the needs of the department as a whole, the institution, and the students. In addition to traditional criteria such as degree attainment, field of research, publication record, and teaching experience, consider including evidence of successful experience mentoring, tutoring, or engaging with diverse populations and other criteria that matter to your department or institution. In later stages of the search process, rely on the consensus you reached to develop job descriptions, announcements, and advertisements; to formulate interview questions; and to structure your evaluation of candidates.

Resist the temptation to wait to develop evaluation criteria until after reviewing application materials. Failure to discuss and agree upon desired qualifications *a priori* may hamper the effectiveness of your recruiting activities and increase the possibility that individual search committee members will favor candidates for reasons not necessarily related to the needs of the department or the position (e.g., "I know the advisor," "I graduated from the same program," "I work in a closely related research area") and will develop or give preferential weight to evaluation criteria that benefit favored candidates. Be prepared to counter the argument that "we all know quality when we see it." All too often, nebulous definitions of quality or excellence prime us to recognize quality in those who look and act similar to the majority of members already in an organization and hinder us from seeing excellence in those who differ in some way from the majority.[2] The temptation to rely on such vague, but reportedly recognizable, definitions of merit may arise from a desire to save time. However, failure to take the time to discuss the needs of the position and the desired qualities of the applicants during the early stages of the search process may compromise the efficiency and effectiveness of the search at later stages. In the absence of a well-developed consensus about qualifications, the pool of applicants you attract may not meet your expectations and the committee's evaluation of candidates may become contentious.

---

2. Madeline E. Heilman, "Description and Prescription: How Gender Stereotypes Prevent Women's Ascent Up the Organizational Ladder," *Journal of Social Issues* 57;4 (2001): 657-674.

Anticipating problems

Despite good faith efforts to gain the support and active involvement of all search committee members, meetings and search activities may not proceed as smoothly or effectively as desired. It may help to anticipate problems and think about how to resolve them. Seek advice from your department chair or from past search committee chairs and members. Some common problems that former search committees have identified, along with resources that may help overcome them, are listed below:

1. **Resistance to efforts to enhance diversity**

   - Allow all members of the search committee to voice their opinions and participate in a discussion on diversity and the search committee's roles and responsibilities related to recruiting and evaluating a diverse pool of applicants.

   - Rely on the materials in Elements II and III of this guidebook to help facilitate this discussion of diversity and to respond to resistance.

   - Consider inviting someone with expertise on research documenting the value of diversity to your committee meetings (e.g., a representative of your institution's equity and/or diversity committee, a staff member of the campus equity and/or diversity office, or a prominent scholar on your campus who conducts research in this field).

   - Remind the search committee that they represent the interests of the department as a whole and, in a broader context, the interests of the university or college.

   - Stress that failure to recruit and fairly evaluate a diverse pool of applicants may jeopardize the search; that it may be too late to address the issue when (or if) you are asked, "Why are there no women or minorities on your finalist list?"

2. **One member dominates the meetings**

   - Review or establish ground rules that encourage participation from all members.

   - Implement the following advice from the "Dominant Participants" section of the UW–Madison Office of Quality Improvement and Human Resource Development's web resource, How to Lead Effective Meetings: http://go.wisc.edu/l52jiy.

     o Structure the committee's discussions by carefully framing questions to solicit multiple viewpoints. For example, instead of asking a very general question such as, "what you do think of the applications we have received?" ask each member to address a more specific question such as, "what are the strengths of each application received?" Very general questions invite wide-ranging, open-ended discussions that provide opportunities for highly verbal and/or opinionated individuals to control the direction of the conversation.

     o If someone is dominating the discussion, acknowledge and briefly summarize his or her viewpoint and then ask for alternative viewpoints from other members.

     o If necessary, talk privately with the individual about the importance of providing other committee members with opportunities to participate in discussions.

3. **Power dynamics of the group prevent some members from fully participating**
   Although a search committee composed of a diverse group of individuals is recommended for its ability to incorporate diverse views and perspectives into your search, it is important to recognize that this diversity also poses challenges. Differences in the status and power of

the members of your search committee may influence their participation. Junior faculty members, for example, may be reluctant to disagree with senior faculty members who may later evaluate them for tenure promotion. Minority and/or women search committee members may not be comfortable if they are the only members of the search committee who advocate for applicants from underrepresented groups. Search committee chairs should evaluate the committee's interactions to assess whether power imbalances are influencing the search and search committee members should bring their concerns about any power imbalances to the chair. Suggestions for improving group dynamics include:

- Review or establish ground rules that encourage participation from all members.

- Hold private conversations with relevant members of the search committee to discuss the role they can play in creating and improving group dynamics.

- Account for varying styles of participation by relying upon a range of forums in which committee members can communicate their thoughts. For example, instead of calling for general discussion of a question, proceed around the table giving each member an opportunity to speak, or ask the committee to take a few minutes to think about and/or write down their thoughts before opening up the conversation.

- If you notice that a member of the committee does not speak at all, you might talk with them after the meeting and mention that you are grateful that they are donating their time. Ask if they feel comfortable in the meeting and ask if you can do anything to facilitate their participation. This may be particularly important if your committee has a student member who is intimidated by having to speak in a room full of faculty.

- For more ideas about encouraging quiet members to share their views, see the "Silent Participants" section of the UW–Madison Office of Quality Improvement web resource, *How to Lead Effective Meetings*: http://go.wisc.edu/x3ityy.

Concluding meetings

1. **Assign specific tasks to committee members**
   For example, the chair could ask each committee member to:

   - list a specified number of qualities they would like to see in an ideal candidate
   - write or review a job description, announcement, or advertisement
   - identify or contact a specified number of sources who can refer potential candidates
   - suggest a certain number of venues for posting job announcements
   - review a specified number of applications

2. **Remind committee members of their assigned tasks**
   Before the next meeting, the chair should remind committee members of their assigned tasks. Committee members should accept responsibility for completing their assignments and be prepared to report on their activities at the next meeting.

3. **Hold committee members accountable**
   The chair should ask each committee member to report on his or her search activities at every committee meeting.

II. ACTIVELY RECRUIT AN EXCELLENT AND DIVERSE POOL OF APPLICANTS

Discussing Diversity and Excellence

Opening the discussion

Diversity is an issue that inevitably surfaces in every search. The diversity of a college or university's faculty and staff influences its strength and intellectual personality. At the campus level as well as at the departmental level, we need diversity in discipline, intellectual outlook, cognitive style, and personality to offer students the breadth of ideas that constitutes a dynamic intellectual community. Diversity of experience, age, physical ability, religion, race, ethnicity, and gender also contribute to the richness of the environment for teaching and research and provide students and the public with colleges and universities that reflect the society they serve.

All too often, initial conversations about diversity and excellence frame these two categories as oppositional—as though one must sacrifice diversity to achieve excellence or compromise excellence to achieve diversity. An alternative viewpoint, as indicated above, is that diversity is a central component of excellence; one cannot achieve excellence without also incorporating diversity. Academia recognizes the importance of diversity in many ways. Departments, for example, typically include faculty members of various ranks and ages who specialize in a broad range of fields within the discipline, and who received their degrees from a variety of institutions. The excellence of a department that does not include faculty experts in a sufficiently broad range of fields would be questionable. The breadth of perspectives offered by a department whose faculty members all graduated from the same institution, no matter how excellent, would be suspect. Indeed, many universities are reluctant to hire their own graduates because they believe that faculty members who trained elsewhere will help foster new ideas, broader perspectives, and creative thinking. Acknowledging that such elements of diversity are critical for attaining excellence can help search committee and departmental members recognize that other types of diversity, such as demographic diversity, are equally important.

In order to build a diverse pool of applicants, it is essential to strive consciously to reach this goal as it may not be achieved by simply advertising an open position. One of the first steps towards developing a commitment to engage actively in efforts to build a diverse applicant pool is to hold an open discussion of diversity at the beginning of the search. **It is too late to address the issue when and if you are asked, "Why are there no women or minorities on your finalist list?"** Frequently, search committees answer this question by claiming that "there weren't any women or minority applicants," or "there weren't any good ones." One goal of the search should be to ensure that there are outstanding women and minority scholars in the pool of applicants.

One possible way of initiating conversations about diversity and excellence is to ask search committee members to articulate their reasons for why it is important to recruit a diverse pool of applicants. In addition to their own experiences and opinions, they can rely upon a large and growing body of research documenting the importance of diversity to excellence. This research illustrates that diversity enriches the education, mentoring, and support students receive, expands and strengthens the curriculum, and enhances research programs.[1]

---

1. A valuable literature review and an extensive annotated bibliography of research on the impact of diversity on college campuses can be found in Daryl G. Smith et al., *Diversity Works: The Emerging Picture of How Students Benefit* (Washington, D.C.: Association of American Colleges and Universities,

Search committee members can also discuss challenges they may face in achieving a diverse applicant pool. They can critically analyze these challenges to determine if they are based on unwarranted assumptions and they can strategize about methods for overcoming challenges. In her study of recipients of prestigious postdoctoral awards and their experiences in the academic job market, Daryl Smith identifies some of the unwarranted assumptions that can hamper search committees' efforts to recruit excellent and diverse applicant pools. Search committee members can rely on this study to discuss challenges and strategies.[2]

Finally, in discussions about diversity and excellence, **it is important to emphasize that every person hired should know that they were hired because they were the best person for the job.**[3] Generating larger and more diverse pools of applicants for every position ensures that the best candidate is actually in the pool and increases the chances that, more often than in the past, the best candidate for the position will be a woman, a person with a disability, or a member of a minority group.

Common views on diversity in hiring—and some responses

When discussing diversity in the hiring process, previous search committee chairs and members have sometimes heard the following, or similar, statements from their colleagues. Members of your search committee or your department may raise these views during your discussions. Some suggestions for responding to such statements are provided below:

"I am fully in favor of diversity, but I don't want to sacrifice quality for diversity."
No one recommends or wants to sacrifice quality for diversity. Indeed, no qualified minority or woman candidate wants to be considered on the basis of diversity alone. The search committee should not only be responsible for finding and including highly qualified minority and female candidates, but also for ensuring that the candidates and the department, college, and university in general know that they were selected on the basis of merit.

1997). See also Scott E. Page, *The Difference: How the Power of Diversity Creates Better Groups, Firms, Schools, and Societies* (Princeton, NJ: Princeton University Press, 2007); Mitchell J. Chang, Daria Witt, James Jones, and Kenji Hakuta, eds., *Compelling Interest: Examining the Evidence on Racial Dynamics in Colleges and Universities* (Stanford, CA: Stanford University Press, 2003); Caroline Sotello Viernes Turner, *Diversifying the Faculty: A Guidebook for Search Committees* (Washington, D.C.: Association of American Colleges and Universities, 2002), 1–2; and Congressional Commission on the Advancement of Women and Minorities in Science, Engineering and Technology Development (CAWMSET), *Land of Plenty: Diversity as America's Competitive Edge in Science, Engineering and Technology* (Arlington, VA: National Science Foundation, September 2000), 1, 9–13.

2. Daryl G. Smith, Lisa E. Wolf, and Bonnie E. Busenberg, *Achieving Faculty Diversity: Debunking the Myths* (Washington, D.C.: Association of American Colleges and Universities, 1996). See also Daryl G. Smith, "How to Diversify the Faculty," *Academe* 86;5 (2000): 48–52.

3. For a discussion of the potential negative consequences of "affirmative action" and how these can be reduced by focusing on the centrality of merit in the decision-making process see: Madeline E. Heilman, Michael C. Simon, and David P. Repper, "Intentionally Favored, Unintentionally Harmed? Impact of Sex-Based Preferential Selection on Self-Perceptions and Self-Evaluations," *Journal of Applied Psychology* 72;1 (1987): 62–68 and Madeline E. Heilman, William S. Battle, Chris E. Keller, and R. Andrew Lee, "Type of Affirmative Action Policy: A Determinant of Reactions to Sex-Based Preferential Selection?" *Journal of Applied Psychology* 83;2 (1998): 190–205. See also Virginia Brown and Florence L. Geis, "Turning Lead into Gold: Evaluations of Men and Women Leaders and the Alchemy of Social Consensus," *Journal of Personality and Social Psychology* 46;4 (1984): 811–824.

"We have to focus on hiring the 'best.'"

True. But what is the best? If we do not actively recruit a diverse pool of applicants, how will we know we have attracted the best possible candidates to apply? What are the criteria for the "best?" What is "best" for the department? The university? The students? Diverse faculty members will bring new and different perspectives, interests, and research questions that can enhance knowledge, understanding, and academic excellence in any field. Diverse and excellent faculty members can help attract and retain students from underrepresented groups. Diverse faculty members can enhance the educational experience of all students— minority and majority. Interacting with diverse faculty offers all students valuable lessons about society, cultural differences, value systems, and the increasingly diverse world in which we live.

"Campuses are so focused on diversifying their faculties that heterosexual white males have no chance," or "Recruiting women and minority faculty diminishes opportunities for white male faculty."

A study examining the experiences of scholars who earned doctorates and won prestigious fellowships (Ford, Mellon, and Spencer) found no evidence of discrimination against white men. Indeed, white men who had some expertise related to diversity had a significant advantage in the job market.[4] As reported in *The Chronicle of Higher Education*, 78% of full-time tenured or tenure-track faculty at American colleges and universities are white and approximately 62% are male.[5]

"There are no women or minorities in our field, or no qualified women or minorities."

Though women and minority applicants may be scarce in some fields, it is rarely the case that there are none. The search committee, as part of its efforts to build its pool, must actively seek qualified women and minority applicants. It may help to present actual data on the numbers and percentages of women and minority PhD recipients in your discipline. Such data are available for many fields (science and non-science) from the National Science Foundation's (NSF) "Survey of Earned Doctorates (SED)" available on its SED Tabulation Engine (https://ncses.norc.org/NSFTabEngine) or from various professional organizations. In addition, many schools, organizations, and individuals are actively working to increase the pool of qualified women and minority scholars and search committee members can support these efforts by contacting such individuals and organizations for assistance in recruiting job applicants.

"How could someone with a disability possibly keep up with the demands of a faculty position?"

The fact that a person with a disability acquired the educational credentials needed for this position demonstrates that the individual, like all similarly qualified applicants, is capable of meeting the requirements for the position. We all know faculty members with disabilities who are performing at the highest levels in their disciplines. Furthermore, research findings

---

4. Smith, *Achieving Faculty Diversity*, 4, 65-70.

5. "Number of Full-Time Faculty Members by Sex, Rank, and Racial and Ethnic Group, 2007," *Almanac of Higher Education, 2010; Chronicle of Higher Education*, August 24, 2009, http://chronicle.com/article/Number-of-Full-Time-Faculty/47992/, accessed 9/10/2012.

show that employees with disabilities are just as dependable and productive as are employees without disabilities.[6]

"The scarcity of faculty of color in the sciences means that few are available, those who are available are in high demand, and we can't compete."

A study of recipients of prestigious Ford Fellowships, all of whom were members of underrepresented minority groups, showed that most of them, 54%, were not aggressively pursued for faculty positions despite holding postdoctoral research appointments for up to six years after finishing their degrees.[7] Only 11% of scholars of color were simultaneously recruited by several institutions. Thus, the remaining 89% of highly qualified minority candidates were not involved in "competitive bidding wars."[8]

"Minority candidates would not want to come to our campus."

The search committee should not make such decisions for applicants, but should let the applicants decide if the campus and/or community is a good match for them. At later stages of the search process, the search committee should show final candidates how they might fit into the campus, provide them with resources for finding out more about the campus and community, and help them make connections to individuals and groups with shared backgrounds and interests. Your institution's equity and/or diversity office, or other campus organizations, can help make these connections.

Tips and Guidelines for Building a Diverse Pool of Applicants

To reach a broad array of excellent and diverse applicants, successful search committees need to implement active recruitment strategies. The typical route of placing an advertisement and waiting for applications is no longer sufficient. Some of the best candidates may not see your advertisement or may not see themselves in your advertised position without some encouragement. Some of the best candidates may not even be actively engaged in a job search.

Departments frequently give attention to recruiting faculty applicants only when they have an open position. Yet successful hiring often depends not only on short-term recruitment strategies that aim to fill an available position, but also on long-term strategies for building and developing a diverse professional network that will assist with future recruiting efforts. Both of these distinct recruitment activities are discussed below.

Active recruiting for an open position

1. Develop a broad definition of the position

Define the desired scholarship, experience, disciplinary background, and expertise required for the position as broadly as possible. Narrowly defined searches may not only exclude

---

6. Sophie L. Wilkinson, "Approaching a Workplace for All: Chemists with Disabilities Profit from a Mix of Pragmatism and Assertiveness on the Job," *Chemical & Engineering News* 79;46 (2001): 55-59; Brigida Hernandez and Katherine McDonald, eds., *Exploring the Bottom Line: A Study of the Costs and Benefits of Workers with Disabilities,* (Chicago, IL: DePaul University and the Illinois Department of Commerce and Economic Opportunity, 2008). See also: Rebecca Raphael, "Academe is Silent about Deaf Professors," *Chronicle of Higher Education* 53;4 (2006): 56.

7. Smith, *Achieving Faculty Diversity*, 4, 95.

8. Smith, *Achieving Faculty Diversity* as cited in Turner, *Diversifying the Faculty*, 16.

women or minority applicants because of pipeline issues, but may also limit your ability to consider individuals with different profiles who, nonetheless, qualify for your position. Be very clear about what is actually "required" and what is "preferred." If appropriate, use "preferred" instead of "required," and "should" instead of "must," when describing qualifications and developing criteria. Pay close attention to the language you use in describing the position and your preferred qualifications. Research indicates that if the position description or qualifications rely heavily on terminology closely associated with stereotypically masculine attributes (e.g., competitive, aggresive, forceful), women may be less interested in applying for the position. More gender-neutral terminology (e.g., accomplished, successful, committed), can often be used instead.[9] **Use this broad definition of the position to advertise or announce your job opening and to develop evaluation criteria.** A carefully crafted job description can help you attract and fairly evaluate a diverse pool of applicants. See **"Resources for Writing a Job Description,"** pp. 25-26.

2. **Expand your evaluation criteria to include aspects of diversity**
   Consistent with your institution's commitment to foster a diverse and inclusive intellectual environment, consider including among your preferred criteria factors such as:

   - Experience working with, teaching, or mentoring diverse groups or diverse students.
   - Ability to contribute to fostering diversity of the campus, curriculum, and/or discipline.

3. **Comply with U.S. Department of Labor requirements for hiring non-U.S. citizens**
   Ensure that your advertisements comply with U.S. Department of Labor (DOL) requirements for hiring non-U.S. citizens. In the event that your search committee selects a non-U.S. citizen as the best candidate for an available position, your institution will only be able to hire that candidate if your search process meets DOL requirements. These requirements are designed to ensure that U.S. citizens have had the opportunity to apply for the position, that the person selected is more qualified than applicants with U.S. citizenship, and that the salary offered to the selected applicant is commensurate with typical salaries for the position. To meet these requirements, the advertisement must:

   - List the job title, minimum qualifications for the position, and principal duties or responsibilities.
   - Be published in a website or publication that is national in scope (websites or publications that list job opportunities only in a specific region may not be sufficient).
   - Be published in a print or electronic version of a professional journal, meaning that in addition to job opportunities the journal regularly publishes articles with scholarly or professional content in either electronic or hardcopy formats.

   Advertisements placed on websites that only list job openings and do not publish scholarly or professional content do not meet DOL requirements.

   In addition, electronic advertisements must be posted for a minimum of 30 calendar days and the start and end dates must be documented. Ideal forms of documentation are computer printouts, including the URL and date, of the advertisement printed from a web browser

---

9. Danielle Gaucher, Justin Friesen, and Aaron C. Kay, "Evidence that Gendered Wording in Job Advertisements Exists and Sustains Gender Inequality," *Journal of Personality and Social Psychology* 101;1 (2011): 109-128.

on the first and last day the ad was posted. For print ads, tear sheets are the preferred form of documentation.

For more information on the process of acquiring approval to hire a non-U.S. citizen, contact your institution's Human Resources office.

4. **Develop an active recruitment plan**
See "Resources" on pp. 26–33 and online at:
http://wiseli.engr.wisc.edu/recruitingresources.php.

- **Advertise not only in the standard journals in your field, but also in publications targeted to women and underrepresented minority scholars in your discipline.**

- **Identify fellowship programs in your field—especially those that aim to expand the representation of women and members of minority groups in the professoriate.** Contact administrators of these programs and seek their assistance in announcing your position. They are particularly well positioned to help you because the programs they administer aim specifically to expand the diversity of the pool of candidates eligible for faculty positions.

- **Make lists of professional meetings, professional societies or associations, and members of these organizations,** and use them to recruit applicants.

- **Identify committees, caucuses, or individuals in your professional societies that work to increase the representation of women and members of minority groups in your discipline.** Solicit their assistance in advertising your position.

- **Contact your alumni/alumnae** and seek their assistance in recruiting applicants for your position.

- **Make calls and send e-mails or letters** to a wide range of contacts asking for potential candidates. Ask specifically for recommendations of women or diverse applicants.

- **Make an effort to identify colleagues with diverse backgrounds or experiences.** Such colleagues may help you reach highly qualified minority or women candidates.

- **Call potential applicants directly** to encourage them to apply. Whenever possible, begin your conversation by referring to the person who recommended that you contact them.

- **Actively involve all search committee members in specific tasks.** For example, each member of the search committee can call ten colleagues to request recommendations of potential candidates and can ask specifically for recommendations of candidates who are women or members of underrepresented minority groups.

5. **Remember that your goal at this point is to EXPAND your pool of applicants**
Achieving an excellent pool of applicants that is more diverse than it has been in the past requires trying strategies you may not have used before and reaching out to individuals, organizations, and institutions you may not have contacted previously. Approach this task as broadly and inclusively as possible, and save sifting and winnowing of applicants for later in the process.

Building and developing diverse professional networks

Most job seekers are aware that successful networking is the most effective means of gaining employment. Networking is also an effective means of recruiting job candidates. To recruit applicants from underrepresented groups successfully, it is essential for department members to develop professional networks that include scholars from underrepresented groups. Faculty members who build such relationships will not only enhance recruitment efforts, but will also help make their discipline more welcoming and inclusive of diverse members and can enrich their own scholarly work by gaining new perspectives on and ideas for their research and teaching. Some advice for expanding and creating inclusive professional networks follows.

1. **Faculty members attending conferences or annual meetings can recruit for the department by engaging in the following behaviors:**

   - **Make conscious efforts to establish collegial relationships with women and minority scholars attending the event.**
     Faculty members attending conferences frequently interact primarily with others they already know well—colleagues from graduate school or people they have served with on committees or panels. Minority scholars and women who are underrepresented in a discipline often report feeling isolated at large annual meetings. Faculty members who make an effort to expand their professional networks by introducing themselves to women and minority members of their organization and learning about their research and teaching interests not only help to make the organization more welcoming and inclusive, but also gain valued colleagues. Such relationships can benefit all parties as they may lead to opportunities for students, research collaboration, teaching innovations, and the sharing of ideas and concerns. They can also be helpful when recruiting for faculty positions because these new colleagues may be able to recommend potential applicants who belong to underrepresented groups.

   - **Establish collegial relationships with promising women and minority graduate students who present papers or posters at the event.**
     Faculty members who attend poster sessions and presentations by graduate students can identify promising students, introduce themselves, and learn more about the students' research and teaching interests. Many faculty members already do this for majority students and/or students of their established colleagues, but are more hesitant about approaching women, minority students, or students with a disability. Those who take the initiative to introduce themselves to women and minority students, show genuine interest in their work, communicate with them periodically, and maintain contact at subsequent conferences will be far more successful in recruiting them to apply for an open faculty position or in establishing a collegial relationship with them if they are hired at a different institution.

   - **Represent the department at meetings of caucuses or subcommittees for women and/or minority scholars or attend open sessions held by or for such caucuses and subcommittees.**

2. **Ensure that women and minority scholars are well-represented among speakers invited to deliver departmental colloquia or seminars**
   Departmental colloquia or seminars provide excellent opportunities to familiarize departmental members with the work and research of scholars outside their own institution, provide networking opportunities for faculty and students, and allow visitors to become better acquainted with your department, campus, and community. By consistently including women and minority scholars among invited speakers, departments can expand their professional networks and rely on a broader and more diverse pool of scholars when recruiting applicants for available positions.

3. **Establish professional relationships with colleagues and related departments at institutions with a good record of graduating women or minority PhD students**

   Such institutions may include Historically Black Colleges and Universities, institutions with high or predominantly Hispanic enrollment, and institutions enrolling 50% or more minority students. The U.S. Department of Education provides a list of these institutions: www.ed.gov/about/offices/list/ocr/edlite-minorityinst-list.html. *Diverse Issues in Higher Education* publishes an annual report ranking institutions on their graduation of minority students. These rankings are available online at: http://diverseeducation.com/top100.

4. **Maintain contact with your alumni/alumnae**

   Maintaining good relationships and contact with your alumni/alumnae, especially those who belong to underrepresented groups, can provide you with access to their growing professional networks. They can recommend potential applicants to you and can serve as effective ambassadors for your department, college, or institution.

Dispense with assumptions that may limit your efforts to recruit actively and broadly

Previous search committee chairs report that the following assumptions may hamper efforts to recruit a diverse and excellent pool of candidates. Some potential responses to these assumptions are included below.

"We shouldn't have to convince a person to apply."

In fact, many of the finalists in searches across campus—for positions as diverse as assistant professor, provost, and chancellor—had to be convinced to apply. Some candidates may think their credentials do not fit, that they are too junior, or that they don't want to live in your community. Talk to prospective applicants and ask them to let the committee evaluate their credentials. Remind them that without knowing who will be in the pool, you cannot predict how any given applicant will compare and ask them to postpone making judgments themselves until a later time in the process. Once they are in the pool, either side can decide that the fit is not a good one, but if applicants don't enter the pool, the committee loses the opportunity to consider them. Another argument to use with junior colleagues is that the application process will provide valuable experience even if their application is unsuccessful in this search. Remind them that going through the process will make them more comfortable and knowledgeable when the job of their dreams comes along. Individual attention and persistence pay off—there are many examples from other searches of "reluctant" applicants who needed to be coaxed into the pool and turned out to be stellar finalists.

"Any worthy candidate knows to look for job listings in Journal X."

Not all potential applicants are necessarily engaged in an active job search. Some may be employed in a temporary position, others may be planning to complete another year of a post-doctoral position, and others simply may not have considered your institution as a good fit for them. Seeing your job opening listed in a publication or on a listserv targeted to their specific group may help women and minority scholars see themselves as potential members of your institutions. Personal contact with a member of your committee may convince scholars who would not otherwise have done so to consider applying for your position.

"Excellent applicants need the same credentials as the person leaving the position."

There are many examples of highly successful people who have taken nontraditional career routes. Some of our best faculty were recruited when they had less than the typical amount of postdoctoral experience, were employed at teaching colleges, had taken a break from their careers, or were working in the private sector or in government positions. At the national level, it is interesting to note that many women deans of colleges of engineering in the U.S., especially those who became deans in the 1980s and 1990s, did not follow the traditional path of serving as department chair before becoming dean.[10] Think outside the box and recruit from unusual sources. You can always eliminate applicants from the pool later.

"People from Group X won't fit in here."

We all make assumptions about people based on the university granting their degree, the part of the country or world they come from, and their ethnicity or gender. Encourage your committee members to recognize this and avoid making assumptions. Your search will only be hurt by comments such as: "we only recruit from tier-1 research institutions," "people from the South never adjust to our cold weather," "we never recruit well from the coasts," or "individuals from that culture don't make eye contact and that won't work for our department."

---

10. Peggy Layne, "Perspectives on Leadership from Female Engineering Deans," *Leadership and Management in Engineering* 10;4 (October 2010): 185-190.

RESOURCES

Resources for writing a job description

Prepared by Mariamne Whatley for the UW–Madison School of Education's Equity & Diversity Committee, 10/1/97 (with minor adaptions)

The most important point to remember is that whatever is written on the Position Description (PD) is binding! [Check with your own institution regarding its policies for official position descriptions or announcements.]

1. **Title:** List all possible titles. If you list an Assistant Professor title and the top candidate is currently an Associate or Full Professor elsewhere, that person would have to be hired at an Assistant Professor level. The dean must have approved a search that would allow for hiring either at the junior or senior level; that information would have to be clearly stated in the PD.

2. **Proposed salary:** Always give only a minimum salary; that information can be obtained from the chair, who would have consulted with the dean. Do not list a maximum because it may not be possible to change it. If you read the newspapers, you'll know what happens if someone is hired at a salary higher than the listed maximum.

3. **Required qualifications:** This is the heart of the PD and needs to be considered carefully, especially when determining what is **required** and what is **preferred.**

   - Degree: Make sure you don't limit the pool artificially. If you write PhD, then an EdD is not acceptable. The phrase "earned doctorate" gives most flexibility if that is what you require. If other terminal degrees are possible (MFA, for example), be sure to include those options. You also should consider carefully what area that degree should be in, so as not to limit the pool.

   - Teaching or other school experience: Some positions, such as supervising student teachers, may require a minimum number of years of school teaching experience. If this is a requirement, state that. However, if it is not required, state "preferred." If the perfect candidate does not have the **required** experience, you won't be able to hire (or, if it slips by, another candidate could complain and win).

   - In order to give the message that your department values diversity, you might use a phrase such as, "Experience in multicultural education preferred" or "Experience working with diverse populations preferred."

   - You can include a statement such as, "Evidence of potential for developing a significant research program in (field)." This may help prevent some of those totally inappropriate applications all search committees receive and will help in sorting through applications.

RESOURCES

4. **Responsibilities:** It is not necessary to go into minute detail. However, don't leave any area out. An applicant should be aware, for example, that responsibilities include: teaching at the undergraduate and graduate level; advising students; service activities at local, state, and national levels, as well as at the university; research and scholarly productivity of nationally recognized quality. Applicants need to know what they are applying for. As an example, later on, a successful candidate might refer back to the responsibilities and point out that there is no obligation to do service because it isn't listed.

5. **Application procedure:**

- Application package: Decide exactly what you want in an application package, such as C.V., transcripts of graduate work, abstract of dissertation, samples of scholarly writing. If you are only interested in writing samples from the short list applicants, then this should not be listed in the application package.

- Letters of reference: State clearly whether you want three letters of reference sent directly to the search committee or whether they can be included in the package (not a great idea) or if you just want names of referees. The last option can mean a lot of work for the search committee.

- Deadline: Choose a deadline that gives enough time to do the necessary advertising but doesn't push you too close to the end of the hiring season. Faculty searches require a minimum of two months. State what you expect to receive by the deadline, such as complete application package; complete application package plus letters of reference; or letter of application and C.V.

- Time for review of PD: Be sure you allow sufficient time for the PD to be reviewed at all required levels in your institution. Keep in mind that some publications have long lead times for publishing notices of job openings.

6. **Affirmative action and confidentiality statements:** Check with your institution regarding requirements for such statements and for preferred or suggested wording of these statements in advertisements and announcements.

Campus Resources for Building a Diverse Pool of Applicants

1. **Committees or offices for affirmative action or equity and diversity**
   Most universities and colleges have an Office for Affirmative Action and campus-wide or college-specific committees charged with working to achieve equity and diversity goals. Administrators of such offices and committees or their representatives can provide you with valuable assistance. You can consult with them about your search and rely upon them to provide useful information to your committee and to job candidates. They will likely have a list of recruiting resources similar to, or perhaps broader than the resources provided in this guidebook, and will also have knowledge about local resources available to you. Make an

RESOURCES

effort to learn about the infrastructure supporting diversity initiatives on your campus and rely on this support to help you in your search.

2. **Office of Human Resources**
   The Office of Human Resources on your campus is another important resource you can rely on. Many such offices will provide advice and resources for recruiting. They may also produce guidelines or policies regarding the search process on your campus, and they may provide valuable information about your institution and its employee benefits that can help you recruit applicants.

3. **Campus colleagues and organizations**
   Many campuses have formal or informal organizations for women, members of minority groups, and people with disabilities. These organizations may exist to offer mutual support to members, to provide opportunities for socializing, or to advocate on behalf of members. In all cases, these organizations may be willing to use their networks to help you advertise or announce job openings and may help to increase your awareness of resources on campus and in your community that could be of interest to potential job applicants. Also, consult with campus colleagues who are women and/or members of underrepresented groups. They may provide valuable advice, connect you to any organizations to which they belong, and use their own professional networks to aid you in your search.

Online Sources of Information, Research, and Advice

Please note: Before adopting any advice supplied by off-campus organizations, consult with an appropriate campus resource or official to check that your actions are consistent with your institution's policies and procedures. Appropriate resources might include: the campus-wide Office of Human Resources, your school or college's Human Resources Department, the campus Office for Equity and Diversity and/or Affirmative Action, and your legal counsel or Office of Legal Services.

This list of resources is also available on WISELI's website:
http://wiseli.engr.wisc.edu/recruitingresources.php#info

1. **AAUP – American Association of University Professors (www.aaup.org)**
   "The AAUP has a longstanding commitment to increasing diversity in higher education." Its website provides policy statements on diversity, advice, and resources. Documents that are particularly pertinent to efforts to increase faculty diversity include:

   • **Recommended procedures for increasing the number of minority persons and women on college and university faculty**
     (www.aaup.org/AAUP/pubsres/policydocs/contents/AAplans.htm)

RESOURCES

- **Resources on Diversity & Affirmative Action in Higher Education** (www.aaup.org/AAUP/issues/diversity/div-aa-resources.htm)
  This page links to documents describing the Association's policies, research, and analysis on issues of diversity and affirmative action, including:

  How to Diversify Faculty: The Current Legal Landscape (2006) (www.aaup.org/AAUP/issues/diversity/howto-diversify.htm)

  Sources on the Educational Benefits of Diversity (www.aaup.org/AAUP/issues/diversity/edben.htm)

  Diversity Bibliography (www.aaup.org/AAUP/issues/diversity/Diversitybib.htm)

2. **AAC&U – Association of American Colleges and Universities (www.aacu.org)**
   The AAC&U provides national leadership "to advance diversity and equity in higher education." Its web page, "Diversity and Inclusive Excellence" lists initiatives, research publications, and resources relevant to campus diversity initiatives (www.aacu.org/resources/diversity).

3. **AAMC – Association of American Medical Colleges (www.aamc.org)**
   The AAMC's webpage, "Diversity Initiatives: Supporting Medical School Faculty and Administration," provides links to AAMC groups focused on aspects of diversity as well as reports and data on fostering faculty diversity in medical education (www.aamc.org/initiatives/diversity).

4. **NSF – National Science Foundation: Science and Engineering Doctorate Awards (www.nsf.gov/statistics/doctorates)**
   This series of annual reports, based on results from the NSF's Survey of Earned Doctorates, "presents data and trends on doctorates awarded in science and engineering. Information is also available on characteristics of doctorate recipients, institutions awarding doctorates, and post-graduation plans of doctorate recipients." Characteristics of doctoral recipients for which data are available include field of study, sex, race or ethnicity, citizenship status, and disability status. Other NSF reports and resources which may be useful to search committees include:

   - **Doctoral Scientists and Engineers Profiles** (www.nsf.gov/statistics/doctoralprofiles)
   - **Characteristics of Doctoral Scientists and Engineers in the United States** (www.nsf.gov/statistics/doctoratework/)
   - **WebCASPAR and the Survey of Earned Doctorates (SED) Tabulation Engine** (https://webcaspar.nsf.gov and https://ncses.norc.org/NSFTabEngine)

     "The WebCASPAR database provides easy access to a large body of statistical data resources for science and engineering (S&E) at U.S. academic institutions. WebCASPAR emphasizes S&E, but its data resources also provide information on non-S&E fields and higher education in general." WebCASPAR, however, does not include data on gender, citizenship, race, and ethnicity of degree recipients after 2006. The SED Tabulation Engine provides access to such information for degree recipients from 2006 and later. Search committees can use the Tabulation Engine to learn more about the diversity of potential applicant pools.

RESOURCES

Directories of Women and Minority Doctoral Candidates and Recipients

**These and additional resources are also available on WISELI's website:
http://wiseli.engr.wisc.edu/recruitingresources.php#directories**

1. **CIC Doctoral Directory (www.cic.net/Home/Students/DoctoralDirectory)**
    The Committee on Institutional Cooperation (CIC) is "a consortium of the Big Ten universities plus the University of Chicago." It publishes the CIC Doctoral Directory online in an effort "to increase the visibility of doctoral alumni who bring diverse perspectives and experiences to higher education." The searchable directory can help colleges, universities, and other potential employers recruit underrepresented graduates of CIC institutions. The directory lists "American Indians, African Americans, and Latina/Latinos in any field of study [and] Asian Americans in social science and humanities fields." To be eligible for inclusion, "registrants must be a U.S. citizen or Permanent Resident who completed a PhD, MLS, or MFA degrees at one of the CIC member universities."

2. **Rice University NSF ADVANCE Program's National Database of Underrepresented PhD Students and Postdocs (http://advance.rice.edu/nifpdb.aspx)**
    "This searchable database contains application entries and CVs of underrepresented postdoctoral and late stage PhD students in various science, engineering, and psychology fields. The majority of applications were submitted for the NSF-funded ADVANCE Workshop at Rice University: 'Negotiating the Ideal Faculty Position.' Applicants included in the database are those who granted permission to share their information with Rice or non-Rice faculty search committees."

3. **Ford Fellows Directory (http://nrc58.nas.edu/FordFellowDirect/Main/Main.aspx)**
    The Ford Foundation Fellowship Program seeks "to increase the diversity of the nation's college and university faculties by increasing their ethnic and racial diversity, to maximize the educational benefits of diversity, and to increase the number of professors who can and will use diversity as a resource for enriching the education of all students." The Fellowships Office of the National Resource Council maintains a searchable directory of Ford Fellowship recipients. "The directory is searchable by key words including fellowship award year, field of study, fellowship institution, and other data that Ford Fellows elect to share. To date, there are over 2,700 Ford Fellows. This database ... allows universities and other institutions to conduct employment and expertise searches for highly trained and talented academics from diverse backgrounds."

Recruiting and Networking Resources

In addition to advertising in key journals of specific disciplines and in general academic publications such as *The Chronicle of Higher Education* or *Science* and *Science Careers*, it is helpful to advertise in publications targeted toward specific demographic groups. Though women and members of minority groups will undoubtedly see your advertisements in the standard journals for your field, you can increase the likelihood that they will apply for your open positions by

RESOURCES

also advertising in publications for women and minority scholars. Advertising in these publications demonstrates your commitment to conducting a diverse search and may encourage women and minority scholars to regard your institution as place in which they would be welcome.

The resources listed below include the following:

- Publications targeted to women and minority scholars
- Academic organizations with subcommittees or caucuses for underrepresented groups
- Academic organizations that maintain online career centers that enable employers to list job openings and job seekers to post résumés or curricula vitae

In addition to advertising in these publications, posting job openings in online career centers, and searching for qualified candidates in online databases, you can rely on the contact information provided for various societies and organizations, and in some cases for their leaders and members, in your efforts to increase the diversity of your own professional networks.

Resources for all academic disciplines

This list of resources is also available on WISELI's website:
http://wiseli.engr.wisc.edu/recruitingresources.php#all

1. *Diverse: Issues in Higher Education* (http://diverseeducation.com)
   DiverseJobs (http://diversejobs.net)
   Published in print and online, *Diverse: Issues in Higher Education* focuses "on matters of access and opportunity for all in higher education." The "job site" of *Diverse: Issues on Higher Education*, "DiverseJobs," enables employers to post job openings for faculty and university or college administrative positions.

2. **HERC – The National Higher Education Recruiting Consortium**
   (www.hercjobs.org)
   As collaborative associations of universities and colleges, HERC aims to help member institutions work together in "addressing faculty and staff dual career and employment outreach challenges on their campuses." HERCs exist in many regions of the United States and "maintain regional, web-based search engines that include listings for all job openings, both faculty and staff, at all member institutions. "The centrality of job postings and regional resources as well as the website's ability to accommodate dual career searches distinguishes HERC from other employment websites." Member institutions can "post an unlimited number of faculty, staff and executive job listings on the website, and all HERC jobs are cross-posted on the National HERC website and two leading job boards; Indeed.com and Simplyhired.com." A listing of the regional HERCs and links to their websites is available at: www.hercjobs.org.

3. *Hispanic Outlook in Higher Education* (www.hispanicoutlook.com)
   The Hispanic Outlook in Higher Education (H/O) is "a top information news source and the sole Hispanic educational magazine for the higher education community, and those involved in running our institutions of higher learning." Advertising position openings in *H/O* allows employers to reach a highly multicultural audience.

RESOURCES

4. **INSIGHT into Diversity** (www.insightintodiversity.com)

   INSIGHT into Diversity, formerly the *Affirmative Action Register*, aims to connect "professionals with institutions and businesses that embrace a workforce that reflects our world." Their free magazine and online recruitment site serves employers and job seekers in the fields of "higher education, healthcare, government, and business." Employers can post job openings online and in print editions. Job seekers can search for job openings and post their résumés online.

5. **Journal of Blacks in Higher Education** (www.jbhe.com)

   "*The Journal of Blacks in Higher Education* is dedicated to the conscientious investigation of the status and prospects for African Americans in higher education." Employers may post job openings online or advertise in the print edition of the journal.

6. **Latinos in Higher Ed** (www.latinosinhighered.com)

   This web site aims to "promote career opportunities in higher education for the growing Latino population." It connects employers "with the largest pool of Latino professionals in higher education in the United States, Puerto Rico and internationally by disseminating employment opportunities to registered candidates and a national network of Latino-serving organizations and listservs."

7. **Women in Higher Education** (www.wihe.com)

   Women in Higher Education is a monthly news journal that focuses on issues of gender in higher education. It reaches "thousands of talented women leaders on campuses all over the USA, Canada, and worldwide on the internet." Employers can list position openings in print and/or online editions.

Resources for the sciences and engineering (broad disciplinary fields)

This list of resources is also available on WISELI's website:
http://wiseli.engr.wisc.edu/recruitingresources.php#se

1. **AISES – American Indian Science and Engineering Society** (www.aises.org)

   AISES strives "to substantially increase the representation of American Indians and Alaskan Natives in engineering, science, mathematics, and other related technology disciplines." AISES provides an online "Job Board" where employers can post job opportunities (www.aises.org/what/programs/postjobs) and maintains a searchable résumé database (www.aises.org/what/programs/resumedatabase). AISES also publishes a quarterly magazine, *Winds of Change* (www.aises.org/what/woc). As "the premier nationally distributed magazine published with a single-minded focus on career and educational advancement for American Indian and Alaska Native people in STEM," Winds of Change can be a "valuable recruitment tool for corporations, government agencies, tribal and non-tribal businesses, and colleges and universities across the US."

2. **AWIS – Association for Women in Science** (www.awis.org)

   "Dedicated to achieving equity and full participation for all women in science, technology, engineering and mathematics," AWIS provides an online "job bank" (www.awis.org/jobbank.cfm) in which employers can list job openings and view posted résumés, Job announcements can also be advertised in the *AWIS Magazine*.

RESOURCES

3. **Faculty For The Future (www.engr.psu.edu/fff)**
   Faculty for the Future aims to increase the number of women and underrepresented minority faculty in engineering, science, and business. Its website is "dedicated to linking a diverse pool of women and under-represented minority candidates from engineering, science, and business with faculty and research positions at universities across the country." Administered by WEPAN (Women in Engineering ProActive Network), the website allows members of academic institutions to post positions and search submitted résumés. No fee is charged for this service.

4. **SACNAS – Society for Advancement of Chicanos and Native Americans in Science (http://sacnas.org)**
   SACNAS is "dedicated to fostering the success of Hispanic/Chicano and Native American scientists." Institutions may post job announcements online (http://sacnas.org/institutions/advertising/web-ads) and in *SACNAS News* (http://sacnas.org/institutions/advertising/print-ads).

Discipline-specific Resources for the Sciences, Technology, Engineering, Mathematics, and Medicine (STEMM)

For a comprehensive and continuously updated listing of organizations for women and minority scholars in science and engineering, please see our webpage:
http://wiseli.engr.wisc.edu/recruitingresources.php#STEM

These online recruiting resources include links to organizations in many disciplines including, but not limited to:

- Agricultural Sciences
- Astronomy/Astrophysics
- Biological Sciences
- Chemistry
- Engineering
- Mathematics
- Physics
- Medicine
- Nursing
- Pharmacy
- Veterinary Medicine

Many of these organizations maintain online listings of job openings, searchable résumé databases for people actively seeking positions, and listings of women and minority scholars working in their field. Some organizations provide only a list of their officers or members. In addition to posting your position openings and reviewing posted résumés on these websites, we recommend contacting the officers of relevant organizations for women and minority scholars to inform them about your position, seek their advice about recruiting applicants, and ask them to recommend or refer you to potential applicants. Search committee members can rely on membership lists of these organizations as resources as they strive to expand the diversity of their professional networks.

RESOURCES

Resources for the arts, humanities, social sciences and professional schools

The listings above concentrate on resources for women and minority scholars in the sciences and engineering, fields in which women and minority scholars are especially underrepresented. Professional societies in other areas may also maintain similar resources. We recommend contacting the professional societies in your field and any committees for women and minority members of these societies. Contacting these committees and their members can not only help search committees recruit applicants but can also enhance and diversify professional networks.

The online recruiting resources listed on our webpage **(http://wiseli.engr.wisc.edu /recruitingresources.php#etal)** include links to organizations in the following disciplines:

- Anthropology
- Art
- Business
- Classics
- Economics
- History
- Law

- Library Sciences
- Modern Languages
- Philosophy
- Political Science
- Psychology
- Social Work
- Sociology

III. RAISE AWARENESS OF UNCONSCIOUS ASSUMPTIONS AND THEIR INFLUENCE ON EVALUATION OF APPLICANTS

Research on unconscious bias and assumptions

We all like to think that we are objective scholars who judge people solely on merit—on their credentials, the quality of their work, and the nature of their achievements. Copious research, however, shows that a lifetime of experience and cultural history shapes every one of us and our judgments of others.

The results of controlled research studies demonstrate that even people who are strongly committed to egalitarian values and believe that they are not biased can hold implicit or unconscious assumptions that influence their judgments.[1] Examples of such implicit biases include expectations about physical and/or social characteristics associated with race, sex, age, and ethnicity; assumptions about people who are likely to match certain job descriptions or enter specific fields of study; and even attitudes about types of academic institutions and the people they educate and employ.

Listed below are examples from a vast and growing body of literature that demonstrate the role unconscious or implicit biases and assumptions can play in evaluation. It is important to note that in most studies examining evaluation and gender, the sex of the evaluator was not significant; both men and women share and apply the same assumptions about gender.

Learning about these studies can increase your awareness of how biases, attitudes, and other factors not related to job qualifications may influence evaluation of applicants. Recognizing the role that biases and assumptions can play may help reduce their impact on your search and review of applications.

Examples of common social assumptions or expectations

- When shown photographs of people of the same height, evaluators overestimated the heights of male subjects and underestimated the heights of female subjects, even though a reference point, such as a doorway, was provided.[2]

- When shown photographs of men with similar body types, evaluators rated the athletic ability of African American men higher than that of white men.[3]

- When asked to choose counselors from among a group of equally competent applicants who were neither exceptionally qualified nor unqualified for the position, students chose white candidates more often than African American candidates, indicating their willingness to give members of the majority group the benefit of the doubt.[4]

---

1. John F. Dovidio, "On the Nature of Contemporary Prejudice: The Third Wave," *Journal of Social Issues* 57;4 (2001): 829-849; Mahzarin R.Banaji, Max H. Bazerman, and Dolly Chugh, "How (Un)Ethical Are You?" *Harvard Business Review* 81;12 (2003): 56-64.

2. Monica Biernat, Melvin Manis, and Thomas E. Nelson, "Stereotypes and Standards of Judgment," *Journal of Personality and Social Psychology* 60;4 (1991): 485-499.

3. Monica Biernat and Melvin Manis, "Shifting Standards and Stereotype-Based Judgments," *Journal of Personality and Social Psychology* 66;1 (1994): 5-20.

4. John F. Dovidio and Samuel L. Gaertner, "Aversive Racism and Selection Decisions: 1989 and 1999," *Psychological Science* 11;4 (2000): 315-319.

- When rating the quality of verbal skills as indicated by vocabulary definitions, evaluators rated the skills lower if they were told an African American provided the definitions than if they were told that a white person provided them.[5]

These studies show that we often apply generalizations that may or may not be valid to the evaluation of individuals.[6] In the study on height, evaluators applied the statistically accurate generalization that men are usually taller than women to their estimates of the height of individuals who did not necessarily conform to the generalization. If we can inaccurately apply generalizations to objective characteristics as easily measured as height, what happens when the qualities we are evaluating are not as objective or as easily measured? What happens when—as in the studies of athletic ability, verbal ability, and choice of counselor—the generalizations are not necessarily accurate? What happens when such generalizations unconsciously influence our evaluations?

Examples of assumptions or biases that can influence the evaluation of applications

- Researchers developed sets of four résumés for job applicants with "white-sounding" or "African American-sounding" names. Two of the résumés were of higher quality and two of lower quality. After randomly assigning a "white-sounding" or an "African American-sounding" name to each of the higher quality and each of the lower quality résumés, researchers submitted approximately 5,000 résumés to companies advertising job-openings in Boston and Chicago newspapers and analyzed the number of callbacks for interviews each applicant received. Applicants with "white-sounding" names received 50% more callbacks than did equally qualified applicants with "African American-sounding" names. A within-race analysis of responses to applicants with "white-sounding" names showed, as expected, that applicants with higher quality résumés received significantly more callbacks (27% more) than did less qualified applicants. Better-qualified applicants with "African American-sounding names," did not benefit when compared to less qualified applicants with "African American-sounding names." The increase in callbacks they received (8%) was not statistically significant.[7]

- In a laboratory experiment, 192 participants (84 men and 108 women) evaluated pairs of equally qualified job applicants who were of the same sex and race, but differed on parental status. When assessing pairs of women, evaluators judged mothers to be less committed to their careers and less competent than non-mothers and recommended substantially more non-mothers (84%) than mothers (47%) for hire. When mothers were recommended for hire, their recommended starting salaries were $11,000 (7.4%) lower than for non-mothers. This "motherhood penalty" applied to both white and African American mothers. Evaluators who assessed application materials for pairs of men judged fathers and non-fathers to be equally competent, but deemed fathers to be more committed to their careers than non-fathers, were more likely to recommend fathers than

---

5. Biernat and Manis, 1994.

6. William T. Bielby and James N. Baron, "Men and Women at Work: Sex Segregation and Statistical Discrimination," *American Journal of Sociology* 91;4 (1986): 759-799.

7. Marianne Bertrand and Sendhil Mullainathan, "Are Emily and Greg More Employable than Lakisha and Jamal? A Field Experiment on Labor Market Discrimination," *American Economic Review* 94;4 (2004): 991-1013.

non-fathers for hire, and recommended higher starting salaries for fathers. This study suggests that women on the job market suffer penalties for being parents, while men benefit. In a follow-up audit study to determine whether conditions in actual job markets replicated laboratory findings, researchers responded to newspaper advertisements for entry-level and mid-career positions in marketing and business by submitting application materials for pairs of equally qualified applicants of the same sex, only one of whom was a parent. They sent 1,276 applications to 638 employers over an 18-month period. Analysis of callbacks for interviews showed that "the motherhood penalty" persisted in actual employment settings. Non-mothers received approximately twice as many invitations to interview than did mothers. The difference in responses to fathers and non-fathers was not significant.[8]

- Beginning in the 1970s, symphony orchestras changed their audition policies in an attempt to overcome a bias that favored hiring students of an elite group of teachers. The changes included advertising positions more openly and broadly thereby increasing the number of applicants, adding sitting members of the orchestra to the audition committee, and using a screen designed to conceal candidates' identities from the audition committee. Because the proportion of women hired by symphony orchestras increased substantially in the 1970s and 1980s, researchers examined the records of orchestra auditions to determine whether the adoption of "blind" auditions influenced the evaluation and hiring of women musicians or whether other factors, including a larger pool of female candidates graduating from music schools, played a role. After extensive analysis, the researchers concluded that using a screen to conceal candidates' identities explained one-third of the increase in the proportion of women among newly hired orchestra members. Blind auditions, they argued, fostered impartiality by preventing assumptions that women musicians have "smaller techniques" and produce "poorer sound" from influencing evaluation. Another one-third of the increase in women hired resulted from increased numbers of women in the applicant pool. This finding highlights the importance of recruiting a diverse and excellent applicant pool.[9]

- Research shows that we frequently describe and expect women to be kind, nice, and sympathetic. While individual women may differ in the extent to which they adhere to these gender norms, these are widely held assumptions about women as a group. Similarly, we describe and expect leaders to be commanding, aggressive, competitive, and ambitious. Though we increasingly expect leaders to be collaborative and to be good communicators (often assumed to be female qualities), our assumptions about leaders generally align most closely with our descriptions and expectations of men—perhaps because most leaders have been and continue to be men. Substantial research demonstrates that this incongruity between our perceptions of female gender roles and leadership roles can influence the evaluation of women as leaders; it can cause evaluators to assume that women will be less competent leaders. When women leaders provide clear evidence of their competence, thus violating traditional gender norms, evaluators perceive them to be less

---

8. Shelley J. Correll, Stephen Benard, and In Paik, "Getting a Job: Is there a Motherhood Penalty?" *American Journal of Sociology* 112;5 (2007): 1297-1338.

9. Claudia Goldin and Cecilia Rouse, "Orchestrating Impartiality: The Impact of 'Blind' Auditions on Female Musicians," *American Economic Review* 90;4 (2000): 715-741.

likeable and more hostile and are less likely to recommend them for hiring or promotion.[10]

These studies are just a few examples from a large body of research demonstrating that unconscious assumptions about the competence (or the lack of competence) of women and members of underrepresented groups, implicit expectations about social roles, and common attitudes about personality can and do influence evaluation of job applicants and their experiences on the job market.

Examples of assumptions or biases in academic job-related contexts

Several research studies have shown that biases and assumptions can affect the evaluation and hiring of candidates for academic positions. These studies show that the assessment of résumés and fellowship applications, evaluation of journal articles, and the language and structure of letters of recommendation are influenced significantly by the sex of the person being evaluated.

- In a national study, 238 academic psychologists (118 male, 120 female) evaluated a curriculum vitae for either a junior- or a senior-level applicant. These were actual curricula vitae from an academic psychologist who successfully competed for an assistant professorship and subsequently received tenure early. Researchers randomly assigned a male or a female name to each curriculum vitae. For the junior-level applicant, both male and female evaluators gave the male applicant better evaluations for teaching, research, and service and were more likely to hire the male than the female applicant. At the senior-level, applicant gender did not influence evaluators' decisions to award tenure, but evaluators did raise more doubts about the qualifications of female applicants.[11]

- In a randomized double-blind study, 127 faculty members from highly respected biology, chemistry, and physics departments at three public and three private large, geographically diverse, research-intensive universities in the United States reviewed materials of an undergraduate student applicant for a laboratory manager position. Faculty participants were told that the results of their review would be used to help develop appropriate mentoring programs for undergraduate science students and that students would receive feedback from the review. Researchers randomly assigned a male or female name to the application and asked faculty members to assess the student's competence and hireability, to indicate what starting salary they would provide to the student if hired, and to answer several questions designed to assess the extent of mentoring they would provide to the student. Both male and female faculty participants rated the male applicant as more

---

10. Julie E. Phelan, Corinne A. Moss-Racusin, and Laurie A. Rudman. "Competent Yet Out in the Cold: Shifting Criteria for Hiring Reflect Backlash Toward Agentic Women," *Psychology of Women Quarterly* 32;4 (2008): 406-413; Alice H. Eagly and Linda L. Carli, *Through the Labyrinth: The Truth About How Women Become Leaders* (Boston, MA: Harvard Business School Press, 2007); Madeline E. Heilman, Aaron S. Wallen, Daniella Fuchs, and Melinda M. Tamkins, "Penalties for Success: Reactions to Women Who Succeed at Male Gender-Typed Tasks," *Journal of Applied Psychology* 89;3 (2004): 416-427; Alice H. Eagly and Steven J. Karau, "Role Congruity Theory of Prejudice Toward Female Leaders," *Psychological Review* 109;3 (2002): 573-598; Cecilia L. Ridgeway, "Gender, Status, and Leadership," *Journal of Social Issues* 57;4 (2001): 637-655.

11. Rhea E. Steinpreis, Katie A. Anders, and Dawn Ritzke, "The Impact of Gender on the Review of the Curricula Vitae of Job Applicants and Tenure Candidates: A National Empirical Study," *Sex Roles* 41:7/8 (1999): 509-528.

competent and hireable than the female applicant. They also offered a higher starting salary and more mentoring to the male student.[12]

- A study of over 300 recommendation letters for medical faculty hired by a large U.S. medical school found that letters for female applicants differed systematically from those for males. Letters written for women were shorter, provided "minimal assurance" rather than solid recommendation, raised more doubts, portrayed women as students and teachers while portraying men as researchers and professionals, included fewer superlative adjectives, and more frequently mentioned women's personal lives.[13] A later study comparing 277 recommendation letters for male and female applicants for a faculty position in chemistry and biochemistry at a large research university found fewer differences between letters written for males and females. However, this study upheld the finding that letters written for men included more superlative adjectives than did letters for women—even when qualifications for men and women applicants were equivalent.[14]

- In a study of postdoctoral fellowships awarded by the Swedish Medical Research Council (MRC), researchers compared the publication records of fellowship applicants to the MRC reviewers' assessments of applicants' scientific competency. To assess publication records, researchers calculated a "total impact score" for each applicant based on their total number of publications, number of first-author publications, and on the impact factors of the journals in which they published. For male applicants, the researchers found a linear relationship between "total impact scores" and the competency ratings assigned by the MRC review board; as impact scores increased so did competency ratings. This linear relationship was nonexistent for female applicants. Women applicants with lower "total impact scores" (20-39) received essentially the same competency ratings as women with higher scores (60-99). Only women with the highest "total impact scores" (>99) received higher competency ratings. When comparing competency ratings for men and women applicants with equal impact scores, men consistently received substantially higher competency ratings. Extrapolating from their data, the researchers concluded that a woman needed to be more than twice as productive as a man in order to receive the same competency rating he received.

  Regression analysis to determine if any factors other than applicant gender explained the discrepancy between publication productivity and competency ratings for women showed that a wide variety of factors including nationality, educational background, field of research, and postdoctoral experience played no role. The only other explanatory factor was whether the applicant personally knew a member of the review panel. Despite the fact that such reviewers recused themselves from the panel, the remaining reviewers

---

12. Corinne A. Moss-Racusin et al., "Science Faculty's Subtle Gender Biases Favor Male Students," *Proceedings of the National Academy of Sciences (PNAS)* 109;41 (2012): 16474-16479.

13. Frances Trix and Carolyn Psenka, "Exploring the Color of Glass: Letters of Recommendation for Female and Male Medical Faculty," *Discourse & Society* 14;2 (2003): 191-220.

14. Toni Schmader, Jessica Whitehead, and Vicki H. Wysocki. "A Linguistic Comparison of Letters of Recommendation for Male and Female Chemistry and Biochemistry Job Applicants," *Sex Roles* 57;7/8 (2007): 509-514.

essentially interpreted an applicant's affiliation with a MRC board member as evidence of competence.[15]

- In a replication of a 1968 study, researchers manipulated the name of the author of an academic article, assigning a name that was male, female, or neutral (initials). The 360 college students who evaluated this article were influenced by the name of the author. They evaluated the article more favorably when the author listed was a male than when the author was female. Questions asked after the evaluation was complete showed that bias against women was stronger when evaluators believed that the author identified only by initials was female.[16] In order to prevent such bias from influencing publication of academic articles, some journals have adopted a double-blind review process that conceals the identities of reviewers and authors. A 2008 study of articles published in the journal *Behavioral Ecology* before and after it implemented a double-blind review process found that double-blind reviews led to a significant increase in the publication of articles with a woman as the first author.[17]

Potential influence of unconscious bias and assumptions on your search

As the research studies described above demonstrate, biases and assumptions can impede your efforts to recruit and review an excellent and diverse pool of candidates. Listed below are some common ways biases and assumptions may exert influence over search committee deliberations:

- Women and minority scholars may be subject to higher expectations in areas such as number and quality of publications, name recognition, or personal acquaintance with a committee member. *(Recall the example of the Swedish Medical Research Council.)*

- Candidates from institutions other than the major research universities that have trained most of our faculty may be undervalued. *(Qualified candidates from institutions such as historically black universities, four-year colleges, government, or the private sector might offer innovative, diverse, and valuable perspectives on research and teaching.)*

- The work, ideas, and findings of women or members of minority groups may be undervalued or unfairly attributed to a research director or collaborators despite contrary evidence in publications or letters of reference. *(Recall the biases seen in the evaluation of résumés or curricula vitae for women and minorities.)*

- The competence and ability of women or minority scholars to run a research group, raise funds, and supervise students and staff may be underestimated. *(Recall assumptions about leadership abilities and the results of blind auditions and blind reviews.)*

---

15. Christine Wennerås and Agnes Wold, "Nepotism and Sexism in Peer-Review," *Nature* 387;6631 (1997): 341-343.

16. Michele A. Paludi and William D. Bauer, "Goldberg Revisited: What's in an Author's Name," *Sex Roles* 9;3 (1983): 387-390.

17. Amber E. Budden et al., "Double-Blind Review Favours Increased Representation of Female Authors," *TRENDS in Ecology and Evolution* 23;1 (2008): 4-6.

- Assumptions about possible family responsibilities and their effect on the candidate's career path may negatively influence evaluation of merit, despite evidence of productivity. *(Recall the study on the "motherhood penalty.")*

- Negative assumptions about whether female or minority candidates will "fit in" to the existing environment can influence evaluation. *(Recall studies showing a lack of fit between common expectations about female gender roles and leadership roles.)*

- The professional experience candidates may have acquired through an alternative career path may be undervalued. *(As examples, latecomers to a field may be more determined and committed; industrial or other nonacademic experience may be more valuable for a particular position than postdoctoral experience.)*

- Other possible biases, assumptions, or unwritten criteria may influence your evaluation. *(Some examples include holding a degree from a prestigious research university, recognizing the names of the candidates, and recognizing the names of or knowing the references provided by the candidates. Such candidates are not necessarily the most qualified. Be sure that such factors don't serve to disadvantage highly qualified candidates, especially candidates from diverse backgrounds.)*

Conclusion

We strongly recommend that search committees discuss the research on unconscious or implicit bias and consider the influence bias and assumptions may have on their judgments and deliberations. We also encourage search committee members to share this information about the role bias and assumptions can play in evaluation with other members of their department who will play a role in evaluating applicants for faculty positions. A condensed version of the above material on unconscious bias and assumptions is available in WISELI's brochure, *Reviewing Applicants: Research on Bias and Assumptions* (http://wiseli.engr.wisc.edu/docs/BiasBrochure_3rdEd.pdf).

In addition to learning about the role bias and assumptions can play in evaluation, search committee members can take an online Implicit Association Test (IAT) to investigate the extent to which social stereotypes that are pervasive in our society can influence their own unconscious thoughts and actions. The IAT webpage provides a choice of (1) taking a "demonstration test" designed to illustrate how an individual's unconscious thoughts and consciously endorsed values can diverge, or (2) participating in ongoing research studies on unconscious or implicit bias (https://implicit.harvard.edu/implicit).

Increasing awareness of bias and assumptions and their role in evaluation is an important first step in minimizing their influence. The next section of this guidebook provides additional recommendations for overcoming the influence of unconscious or implicit bias and assumptions.

IV. ENSURE A FAIR AND THOROUGH REVIEW OF APPLICANTS

Minimizing the influence of unconscious bias (pp. 44–54)

Minimizing Bias: What NOT to do
Minimizing Bias: What to do

Logistics for managing the review of applicants (pp. 54–59)

STAGE 1: Selecting applicants who meet minimum qualifications
STAGE 2: Creating the "long short list" of applicants to consider further
STAGE 3: Selecting a "short list" of finalists to interview
STAGE 4: Evaluating the finalists

Resources (pp. 61–71)

Sample forms to help keep track of and communicate with applicants
Sample letters to applicants

Minimizing the influence of unconscious bias

As the research presented in the previous section indicates, unconscious bias and assumptions can influence evaluation despite our best intentions and our commitment to an equitable search process. Our desire to be fair and objective, unfortunately, is not sufficient to ensure a fair and thorough review of applicants. Consequently, this section of the guidebook presents specific strategies for minimizing the influence of bias on evaluation. The strategies we recommend are grounded in research studies that demonstrate the role of specific interventions in overcoming bias. Following the presentation of these evidence-based strategies for minimizing bias, this section provides logistical advice for organizing and managing the evaluation of applications.

Minimizing Bias: What NOT to do

Surprisingly, research indicates that some common strategies may not be effective at minimizing the influence of bias and assumptions. These include:

1. **Suppressing bias and assumptions from one's mind (or trying to)**

   After becoming aware that unconscious bias and assumptions about groups of people can influence the evaluation of individuals, one common approach is to strive consciously to banish biased thoughts from one's mind; to avoid or suppress thoughts about group stereotypes. Paradoxically, research shows that such attempts can backfire. Attempting to suppress a thought can actually reinforce it and may unintentionally increase bias in evaluation.[1]

   In one research study, participants viewed a photograph of a smiling African American male and wrote a short essay describing a typical day in his life. Half of the participants received instructions not to rely on stereotypes in writing the essay. The other half received no such instructions. A pair of judges, blinded to the experimental condition, rated the extent to which the essays reflected stereotypes. They found that participants instructed to suppress stereotypes did indeed show less reliance on stereotypes than those who did not receive these instructions. In a subsequent task, participants read a story about "Donald" and evaluated him on a set of characteristics. Donald's behavior was intentionally ambiguous; it could be described as hostile or merely as assertive. Participants who had previously engaged in stereotype suppression were more likely to interpret Donald's behavior as hostile. Because Donald's race was not specified, researchers argue that these evaluators were no longer consciously striving to suppress racial stereotypes but that their interpretations of Donald's behavior reflected a rebound effect of suppressing stereotypes about African Americans.[2]

   Individuals highly motivated by their own personal commitment to avoid bias may be able to suppress biased thoughts successfully without experiencing a "rebound effect," but only if they can devote sufficient time and attention to the task. Unfortunately, minor distractions, multi-tasking, mood, and/or fatigue—common aspects of modern life—can hamper even the

---

1. Margo J. Monteith, Jeffrey W. Sherman, and Patricia G. Devine, "Suppression as a Stereotype Control Strategy," *Personality and Social Psychology Review* 2;1 (1998): 63-82; C. Neil Macrae, Galen V. Bodenhausen, Alan B. Milne, and Jolanda Jetten, "Out of Mind but Back in Sight: Stereotypes on the Rebound," *Journal of Personality and Social Psychology* 67;5 (1994): 808-817.

2. Nira Liberman and Jens Förster, "Expression After Suppression: A Motivational Explanation of Postsuppressional Rebound," *Journal of Personality and Social Psychology* 79;2 (2000): 190-203.

most motivated individual's ability to control the influence of unconscious and unwanted thoughts.[3]

Despite the risks of engaging in stereotype suppression, at least one group of scholars points out that suppression of biased thoughts is not "necessarily bad." They argue that "in many situations [possibly including the evaluation of job applicants] inhibiting stereotypic thinking is critical." Nevertheless, they caution us to "be aware that these efforts may influence our subsequent social perceptions and behaviors in important and unexpected ways and may occasionally backfire if we lose the motivation or the ability to correct for a suppression-activated stereotype."[4]

Because of the potentially negative effects of relying on suppression of bias, it is critical to adopt strategies for minimizing the influence of bias as described in the section below, **"What to do."**

2. **Relying on a presumably "objective" ranking or rating system to reduce bias**
   Another common method of attempting to avoid the influence of bias is to rely on the objectivity inherent in mathematics and numbers to develop a system of assigning scores or points to applicants' materials and to rely on this "objective" measure to evaluate and compare applicants. Designing and relying on some type of numeric evaluation system can be very helpful in ensuring a fair and equitable process, but this practice in and of itself will not eliminate bias because each assigned score may be subject to bias. Even if the influence of bias on each assessment is minimal, adding these scores or points together can significantly increase the influence of bias. This is precisely what occurred in the evaluation of applications for prestigious fellowships from the Swedish Medical Research Council, a study described in the previous chapter. The complex scoring system evaluators relied on to promote fairness unintentionally magnified slight biases against women applicants.[5] Consequently, it is important to recognize that bias can play a role in assigning points or scores to various elements of applicants' materials and to rely on the advice provided below for minimizing the influence of bias and assumptions.

Minimizing Bias: What to do

1. **Replace your self-image as an objective person with recognition and acceptance that you are subject to the influence of bias and assumptions**
   In a study examining the role of evaluators' image of themselves as objective decision makers, researchers asked evaluators to assume the role of a company executive and to rate an applicant (identified as either Gary or Lisa) for the position of factory manager. Before conducting the evaluation, half of the participants took a brief survey designed to heighten their sense of objectivity. The survey, for example, asked them to assess the degree to which they "objectively consider all the facts" before forming an opinion and the extent to which they were "rational and objective" when making decisions. The other half of participants took this survey after completing their evaluation. Regardless of when they took the survey, most

3. Natalie A. Wyer, Jeffrey W. Sherman, and Steven J. Stroessner, "The Roles of Motivation and Ability in Controlling the Consequences of Stereotype Suppression," *Personality and Social Psychology Bulletin* 26;1 (2000): 13-25; Monteith, Sherman, and Devine, "Suppression as a Stereotype Control Strategy."

4. Wyer, Sherman, and Stroessner, "The Roles of Motivation and Ability," 24.

5. Christine Wennerås and Agnes Wold, "Nepotism and Sexism in Peer-Review," *Nature* 387;6631 (1997): 341-343.

participants (over 88%) believed themselves to be "above average in objectivity." Participants who took the survey after completing their evaluation gave similar evaluations to the male and female applicants. However, participants whose self-image of being objective was heightened by taking the survey prior to the evaluation showed a substantial preference for the male applicant. The researchers suggest that when people believe themselves to be objective, they naturally assume that their thoughts, beliefs, judgments, and decisions are based on an objective analysis of available information and, therefore, do not stop to consider alternative views or the possibility that they may have been influenced by unconscious assumptions and biases prevalent in society.[6]

2. Strive to increase the diversity of your search committee

As discussed in Element I of this guidebook, a committee composed of diverse members can benefit from the variety of perspectives and new ideas each member provides. The presence and active involvement of diverse members of the committee can also improve efforts to recruit excellent and diverse applicants and can influence the evaluation of applicants. Members of diverse groups, however, do not necessarily evaluate applicants differently than do majority members. Rather, their presence alone may influence the responses of their fellow committee members. For example, an experimental study using the Implicit Association Test (IAT) for racial bias demonstrated that implicit bias towards African Americans decreased when an African American rather than a white person administered the test. One possible explanation is that the African American experimenter, an academician in a high-status position, may have provided participants with a powerful example of a counterstereotype and, thus, may have reduced their reliance on unconscious and common assumptions about African Americans. Alternatively, participants in the presence of an African American experimenter may have been more motivated not to exhibit bias or prejudice. Women and underrepresented minority members serving on a search committee may have a similar influence on their majority peers.[7]

3. Strive to increase the representation of women and minority scholars in your applicant pool

Gender assumptions are more likely to have a negative influence on evaluation of women when women represent a small proportion (25% or less) of the applicant pool. In one study researchers asked participants to evaluate one application (that of a woman) for a managerial position (a male-assumed job), but informed them that in order to accurately evaluate the applicant, they needed to have a broader sense of the applicant pool. Hence, the participants reviewed a package of eight applications before evaluating the identified applicant. Researchers varied the proportion of women applicants in the review package. When 25% or fewer of the applicants were women, participants were less likely to recommend the targeted woman applicant for hire and regarded her as less qualified, as having lower potential, and as being "more stereotypically feminine" than when women's representation among the applicants was greater than 25%. These findings suggest that when women are well-represented in the applicant pool and gender is consequently less salient, evaluators are less likely to be influenced by gender stereotypes and more likely to focus on the individual mer-

---

6. Eric Luis Uhlmann and Geoffrey L. Cohen, "'I Think it, therefore it's True': Effects of Self-Perceived Objectivity on Hiring Discrimination," *Organizational Behavior and Human Decision Processes* 104;2 (2007): 207-223.

7. Brian S. Lowery, Curtis D. Hardin, and Stacey Sinclair, "Social Influence Effects on Automatic Racial Prejudice," *Journal of Personality and Social Psychology* 81;5 (2001): 842-855.

its of each woman applicant. Though similar research has not yet been conducted for members of underrepresented minority groups, it is reasonable to extrapolate from these findings and to expect that a greater proportion of minority members in the application pool will cause evaluators to focus more on the qualifications of individuals than on group stereotypes.[8]

4. Develop well-defined evaluation criteria prior to reviewing applications
Ideally, discussion about evaluation criteria should begin at the earliest stages of the search process because identifying criteria will help search committees write effective job descriptions and recruit well-qualified applicants. The committee should continue to discuss and refine their criteria throughout the search process with the goal of reaching agreement about the priority and specific nature of each criterion before beginning to review applications.

Well-defined criteria can help evaluators focus attention on the merits of individual applicants and on the degree to which they meet criteria, whereas abstract or vaguely defined criteria may increase the possibility for unconscious biases and assumptions to influence evaluation.[9] For example, search committees frequently rely on "excellence in research and/or teaching" as criteria for faculty positions. Although these criteria are perfectly acceptable—even necessary—for job announcements or advertisements, they provide search committee members with little guidance for evaluating applicants. To conduct a fair and effective evaluation, search committee members can discuss and develop consensus around some of the following questions:

- What constitutes excellence in research and/or teaching? Is it number of publications, number of citations, innovation of the topic or approach, significance of results, ability to obtain research funding, or prestige of the journal or publisher? Is it courses taught or developed, results of teaching evaluations, success attracting and mentoring students, or innovation of the topic or pedagogy? Is it the prestige of the home institution and current position, or the applicant's accomplishments?

- What other criteria will committee members rely upon—and how will they assess them? (Some examples of evaluation criteria are listed on Sample Form F, p. 67.)

As the committee develops its evaluation criteria, understand that well-defined criteria are not necessarily narrow. Relatively broad criteria not tied to specific qualifications or a narrow specialty will generally lead to a more interesting and diverse list of qualified applicants. The committee will also want to balance its efforts to define evaluation criteria with the need to remain flexible. It is not always possible to think of all potential evaluation criteria. An applicant might bring interesting strengths or attributes to the department other than those originally sought. If such cases appear, reevaluate and possibly modify the review criteria

---

8. Madeline E. Heilman, "The Impact of Situational Factors on Personnel Decisions Concerning Women: Varying the Sex Composition of the Applicant Pool," *Organizational Behavior and Human Performance* 26;3 (1980): 386-395. See also: Jos van Ommeren, Reinout E. de Vries, Giovanni Russo, and Mark van Ommeren, "Context in Selection of Men and Women in Hiring Decisions: Gender Composition of the Applicant Pool," *Psychological Reports* 96;2 (2005): 349-360.

9. Monica Rubini and Michela Menegatti, "Linguistic Bias in Personnel Selection," *Journal of Language and Social Psychology* 27;2 (2008): 168-181; Daniël H. J. Wigboldus, Gün R. Semin, and Russell Spears, "How do we Communicate Stereotypes? Linguistic Bases and Inferential Consequences," *Journal of Personality and Social Psychology* 78;1 (2000): 5-18.

and be sure to apply these revised criteria equitably to all applicants. If necessary, communicate with all applicants to request additional information or supporting materials.

The consensus different committees reach regarding their evaluation criteria will vary depending on the nature of the position, the standards of the institution and/or discipline, and the needs of the department. It is important to recognize that efforts to define criteria more rigorously will probably not result in completely objective standards that committee members can apply universally and equitably to all applicants. Discussions about criteria, however, will provide search committee members with greater clarity regarding the qualifications they prefer. In addition, they will highlight the subjective nature of definitions of excellence and increase the committee's awareness that this subjectivity creates opportunities for the influence of bias and assumptions.[10]

5. **Prioritize evaluation criteria prior to evaluating applicants**
In addition to developing well-defined criteria, deciding upon how to prioritize them before evaluating applicants is critical. Researchers demonstrated this importance in a series of experiments based on evaluating applicants for two positions: a male-assumed job as a police chief, and a female-assumed job as a women's studies professor.

For the position as police chief, researchers developed two descriptions of job applicants. They described one applicant as "streetwise" and the other as "well schooled and experienced in administration." Research participants read a description of a male or a female applicant who was either streetwise or well educated. They rated the applicant on a number of streetwise and educational characteristics, assessed the importance of each of these characteristics for success as a police chief, and made a recommendation to hire or not hire the applicant. Applicant gender did not influence evaluator's ratings of credentials: male and female applicants received equivalent ratings for their educational and streetwise credentials. Nevertheless, evaluators were more likely to recommend hiring the male rather than the female applicant. The discrepancy between evaluators' equitable ratings of credentials and their inequitable hiring recommendations resulted from the way they prioritized credentials to justify hiring the male. Evaluators rated educational credentials as more important when a male applicant possessed them and as less important when a male applicant lacked them, but made no such adjustments for female applicants.

For the position as a women's studies professor, researchers described applicants as having either good academic credentials or significant experience as an activist for women's issues. Results of the study were similar: evaluators' ratings of the credentials of male and female applicants did not differ, but they were more likely to hire the female applicant. Their hiring decisions were influenced by adjusting the importance of credentials in favor of the female applicant. Evaluators judged activist credentials as more important when female applicants possessed them than when they did not, but made no such adjustment for male applicants.

---

10. Madeline E. Heilman and Michelle C. Haynes, "Subjectivity in the Appraisal Process: A Facilitator of Gender Bias in Work Settings," in *Beyond Common Sense: Psychological Science in the Courtroom*, eds. E. Borgida and S. T. Fiske (Malden, MA: Blackwell Publishing, 2008), 127-155; Madeline E. Heilman, "Description and Prescription: How Gender Stereotypes Prevent Women's Ascent Up the Organizational Ladder," *Journal of Social Issues* 57;4 (2001): 657-674.

In a follow-up experiment, researchers asked evaluators to rate the importance of various credentials **before** conducting their evaluations. Under this condition, bias in hiring recommendations was not significant.[11]

This research demonstrates that prioritizing criteria before reviewing applications can prevent search committee members from unintentionally placing greater value on the qualities a "favored" applicant possesses and less value on credentials he or she lacks. The applicant may be "favored" because the committee members know him or her, know his or her major advisor, attended the same graduate programs, share common research interests, or because the applicant is of the same race, sex, or ethnicity as most members of the department.

6. **Engage in counterstereotype imaging**
   Before reviewing applications, each individual member of the committee can strive to minimize the influence of unconscious assumptions about women and minority applicants by engaging in counterstereotype imaging; by taking time to consciously think about successful, highly competent, well-regarded women and minority members in their department, university, and/or discipline. They can remind themselves of the work these people do, of the research and/or teaching they are recognized for, and of the contributions they make to the department, college, university, and/or profession. Research indicates that these conscious thoughts can replace unconscious assumptions, thus minimizing their influence. A series of experiments used a variety of tests that measure unconscious or implicit bias to compare test scores participants received before and after engaging in a counterstereotype imaging task. Results demonstrated that counterstereotype imaging reduced implicit bias.[12]

   Counterstereotype imaging can also operate at the unconscious level. As discussed above, a diverse search committee may help reduce the influence of unconscious assumptions because the presence and participation of women and minority colleagues on the committee may provide majority members with powerful counterstereotype examples. Similarly, the photographs and pictures in the room in which the committee meets to evaluate and interview applicants can serve to provide counterstereotype (or stereotype consistent) images. A room that showcases photographs and pictures representative of the diversity present or desired in the department or the discipline can provide the search committee with counterstereotype examples that may help mitigate the influence of unconscious or implicit bias. A room populated with photographs depicting only majority members of the department or discipline may reinforce such biases.

   Researchers demonstrated this passive and unconscious influence of counterstereotype imaging in an experimental study that compared participants' scores on a test of implicit racial bias before and after viewing (a) pictures of admired black and disliked white public figures, (b) pictures of admired white and disliked black individuals, or (c) pictures of insects and flowers. Participants who viewed pictures of admired black individuals scored significantly lower on the post-intervention test of implicit racial bias, while the scores of those who viewed admired white individuals or insects and flowers did not change much. Researchers repeated this experiment to determine whether counterstereotype imaging was also effec-

---

11. Eric Luis Uhlmann and Geoffrey L. Cohen, "Constructed Criteria: Redefining Merit to Justify Discrimination," *Psychological Science* 16;6 (2005): 474-480.

12. Irene V. Blair, Jennifer E. Ma, and Alison P. Lenton. "Imagining Stereotypes Away: The Moderation of Implicit Stereotypes through Mental Imagery," *Journal of Personality and Social Psychology* 81;5 (2001): 828-841.

tive at reducing implicit age bias. Indeed, they discovered that exposure to pictures of admired elderly people reduced automatic or implicit bias in favor of younger people.[13]

7. **Spend sufficient time evaluating each applicant and minimize distractions**

Several research studies show that evaluators are much more likely to rely on unconscious biases or assumptions when they are pressed for time, engaged in multiple tasks, tired, and/or under stress. Unconscious bias thus serves as a mental shortcut when we cannot devote much time and attention to evaluation.[14] In one such study, participants rated the job performance of police officers (a male-assumed position) under two different conditions. Under conditions of "high attentional demand," participants conducted their evaluation while simultaneously responding to a second unrelated task. These participants also received instructions to complete the evaluation as quickly as possible and a clock that visibly displayed each passing minute was placed in the room. Participants in the "low attentional demand" condition focused only on the evaluation task and received no instructions about speed or time. All participants received a written description of the police officer's work behavior over a period of three days and a brief biography of the officer that included a photograph of either a woman or a man. There was no significant difference in the job performance ratings evaluators under "low attentional demand" gave to male and female officers. However, evaluators who faced "high attentional demand" rated the job performance of male officers as significantly superior to that of female officers. Indeed, male officers received higher performance ratings from evaluators working under "high attentional demand" than they received from evaluators who gave all their time and attention to the task.[15]

This and other studies suggest that evaluators can reduce the influence of bias and assumptions by minimizing distractions and devoting sufficient time to their evaluation tasks. Some helpful practices include:

- Break the evaluation task into several stages (see "Logistics for Managing the Review of Applicants," pp. 54-59).

- Set aside a block/s of time for conducting evaluations.

- Plan to spend at least 15-20 minutes when conducting a **thorough** review of each application. (Note: as suggested in "Logistics for Managing the Review of Applicants" on pp. 54-59, at certain stages applications may be divided between search committee members so that each member is responsible for **briefly** reviewing all applications and **thoroughly** reviewing a designated number of applications. The advice to spend at least 15-20 minutes applies to the thorough review.)

- Conduct evaluations in a quiet space where you will not be disturbed by ongoing conversations or other interruptions.

- Turn off e-mail and/or any other electronic notifications that provide visual or audio alerts that may disrupt your concentration.

---

13. Nilanjana Dasgupta and Anthony G. Greenwald, "On the Malleability of Automatic Attitudes: Combating Automatic Prejudice with Images of Admired and Disliked Individuals," *Journal of Personality and Social Psychology* 81;5 (2001): 800-814.

14. JoAnn Moody, *Rising Above Cognitive Errors: Guidelines for Search, Tenure Review, and Other Evaluation Committees* (JoAnn Moody, www.DiversityOnCampus.com, 2010).

15. Richard F. Martell, "Sex Bias at Work: The Effects of Attentional and Memory Demands on Performance Ratings of Men and Women," *Journal of Applied Social Psychology* 21;23 (1991): 1939-1960.

- Indulge in a sweet drink or a snack. Research shows that low levels of blood glucose can impair efforts of self-control, including control of biased assumptions, but that consuming a glucose drink can strengthen self-control.[16]

8. **Focus on each applicant as an individual and evaluate their entire application package**
Thoroughly evaluate each applicant's entire application. Do not focus too heavily on or be overly influenced by any one element of the application such as the cover letter, the prestige of the degree-granting institution or post-doctoral program, the letters of recommendation, or the applicant's membership in a particular demographic group. Focusing on the entire application provides a fuller picture of the individual applicant and the degree to which he or she meets your criteria. Research indicates that the more job-related information we have about an applicant and the more we focus on the applicant as an individual rather than as a representative member of some group (a group based on race, sex, ethnicity, or even on institutional affiliation), the less likely we are to rely on assumptions and biases.

For example, a meta-analysis of research studies on the role of sex discrimination in hiring demonstrated that studies in which evaluators had more information regarding applicants' qualifications were less likely to find evidence of sex-discrimination than were studies that provided evaluators with less information. The absence of information regarding individuals' qualifications increased evaluators' tendencies to rely on biases and assumptions.[17]

Another study, recently conducted in France, demonstrated that evaluators who focused on individual differences between members of a targeted minority group (Arabs) were less likely to discriminate against a highly qualified job applicant with an Arabic name than evaluators who concentrated on similarities between group members. In the first phase of this study, researchers engaged participants in a memorization task. They asked all participants to examine and memorize pictures of Arab individuals who varied in sex, age, and style of clothing. They advised one third of participants to take notes about differences between individuals in the group and one third to take notes about similarities between group members. One third of participants served as a control group; they received no advice and took no notes. After some distraction tasks, researchers asked participants to evaluate four applicants for a position as a sales representative. One applicant was highly qualified, two were of average quality, and one was clearly weaker. Researchers assigned a male Arabic name to half of the high quality applications and a male French name to the other half. They assigned French names to all remaining applications. When the name on the highly qualified application was French, participants clearly recognized the applicant's superiority and selected him to interview for the position. However, when the name on the highly qualified application was Arabic, only participants who had previously focused on individual differences between Arabic individuals recognized the applicant's superiority and routinely selected him for an interview. Participants in the control group and in the group that focused on group similarities were less likely to invite the applicant with an Arabic name to interview for the position

---

16. Matthew T. Gailliot et al., "Self-Control Relies on Glucose as a Limited Energy Source: Willpower is More than a Metaphor," *Journal of Personality and Social Psychology* 92;2 (2007): 325-336.

17. Madeline E. Heilman, "Information as a Deterrent Against Sex Discrimination: The Effects of Applicant Sex and Information Type on Preliminary Employment Decisions," *Organizational Behavior and Human Performance* 33;2 (1984): 174-186; Henry L. Tosi and Steven W. Einbender, "The Effects of the Type and Amount of Information in Sex Discrimination Research: A Meta-Analysis," *Academy of Management Journal* 28;3 (1985): 712-723.

and evaluated his application as equivalent to that of the less qualified average applicants with French names.[18]

9. Rely upon inclusion rather than exclusion strategies in making selection decisions
When faced with the task of selecting applicants for further consideration in the hiring process, search committees have essentially two strategies for proceeding. They can exclude from further consideration those applicants they evaluate as unqualified, or they can include the applicants they deem qualified. Theoretically, if search committees fairly and equitably evaluate applicants on the basis of their qualifications, both strategies should yield the same set of applicants. Yet, substantial research on decision-making strategies indicates that they do not. Making decisions using exclusion rather than inclusion strategies results in a larger pool of applicants remaining. This occurs because evaluators make more careful and deliberate choices when deciding whom to include.[19]

One research study investigated how biases and assumptions interact with these decision-making strategies. This study examined (1) how assumptions about gender roles and leadership influenced evaluators' decisions about identifying male and female politicians and judges and (2) how assumptions about African Americans and athleticism influenced evaluators' ability to identify black and white basketball players. Participants in the gender study received instructions to select from a list that included equal numbers of male and female names those individuals who were well-known politicians or judges. For each gender, half of the names were those of well-known politicians or judges and half were random names. Researchers instructed half of the participants to "**circle** the names of those who ARE politicians or judges" (inclusion) and half of the participants to "**cross off** the names of those who ARE NOT politicians or judges" (exclusion). Instructions were similar for participants in the race study but the list included the names of an equal number of well-known black and white basketball players.

In both cases, the research demonstrated the expected effect—evaluators using a strategy of exclusion generated substantially larger lists than did evaluators using an inclusion strategy. Using signal detection theory to analyze "hit rates" (correct identifications) and "false alarms" (misidentifications), the authors demonstrated that evaluators who made decisions by exclusion were more subject to the influence of assumptions associating men as leaders and African Americans as basketball players (more misidentifications). This analysis also showed that relying on an exclusion decision-making strategy led evaluators to set a higher standard (fewer correct identifications) for selecting members of stereotyped groups into counter-stereotyped categories (e.g., women as leaders, or white men as basketball players).

Relying on inclusion decision-making strategies, the authors conclude, can help reduce the influence of bias and assumptions not only by reducing our tendency to rely on differential

---

18. Markus Brauer and Abdelatif Er-rafiy, "Increasing Perceived Variability Reduces Prejudice and Discrimination," *Journal of Experimental Social Psychology* 47;5 (2011): 871-881.

19. Kurt Hugenberg, Galen V. Bodenhausen, and Melissa McLain, "Framing Discrimination: Effects of Inclusion Versus Exclusion Mind-Sets on Stereotypic Judgments," *Journal of Personality and Social Psychology* 91;6 (2006): 1020-1031; Ilan Yaniv and Yaacov Schul, "Acceptance and Elimination Procedures in Choice: Noncomplementarity and the Role of Implied Status Quo," *Organizational Behavior and Human Decision Processes* 82;2 (2000): 293-313; Irwin P. Levin, Mary E. Huneke, and J.D. Jasper, "Information Processing at Successive Stages of Decision Making: Need for Cognition and Inclusion-Exclusion Effects," *Organizational Behavior and Human Decision Processes* 82;2 (2000): 171-193.

criteria for underrepresented groups, but also by focusing our attention on individuals' qualifications rather than on our assumptions about characteristics of the group/s to which they belong.[20]

10. **Stop periodically to evaluate your criteria and their application**

Designate specific times during the evaluation process when the committee will pause to assess the effectiveness and implementation of their evaluation criteria. These times might include before finalizing the "long shortlist," before developing the "shortlist," and before selecting final candidates. At these times, the committee and each individual member can consider the following questions:

- Are you consistently relying on the criteria developed for the position?

- Are your criteria appropriate for the position?

- Are you inadvertently relying on unwritten or unrecognized criteria?

- Are you inadvertently, but systematically, screening out women or underrepresented minority applicants?

- Are women and minority applicants subject to different expectations in areas such as numbers of publications, name recognition, or personal acquaintance with a member of the committee or department? *(An effective way to test for this is to perform a thought experiment—to mentally switch the gender or race of the applicant and consider whether expectations and/or judgments remain unchanged.)*

- Are you underestimating the value and qualifications of applicants from institutions other than the major research universities that train most faculty members? *(It is useful to recognize that many highly successful faculty members have followed nontraditional career paths and that qualified applicants from institutions such as historically black universities, four-year colleges, government, or industry might offer innovative, diverse, and valuable perspectives on research and teaching.)*

- Have the accomplishments, ideas, and findings of women or minority applicants been undervalued or unfairly attributed to a research director or collaborators despite contrary evidence in publications or letters of reference?

- Are you underestimating the ability of women or minority scholars to run a research group, raise funds, and supervise students and staff of differing gender, race, or ethnicity?

- Are assumptions about possible family responsibilities and their effect on an applicant's career path negatively influencing evaluation of an applicant's merit, despite evidence of productivity?

- Are negative assumptions about whether women or minority applicants will "fit in" to the existing environment influencing evaluation?

- Are you evaluating applicants on the basis of promise or potential rather than on evidence of accomplishments and productivity? *(The research discussed above strongly suggests that judgments about promise or potential are particularly susceptible to the influence of bias and assumptions.)*

---

20. Hugenberg, Bodenhausen, and McLain, 2006.

11. Be able to defend every decision

Each member of the search committee should be able to defend cogently every decision to accept or reject an applicant at each stage of the search process. The reasons they provide should be based on evidence in the applicant's record and performance and on the criteria established for the position. It is particularly important to hold reviewers accountable not only for the competence of the applicants they recommend for hire, but also for the fairness and equity of their review.

Research shows that holding evaluators accountable only for the competence of the applicants they select may lead them to assume that applicants who resemble those who have previously succeeded in the position are the most competent or the best choice. Under such conditions, evaluators may assume that applicants who differ from the majority previously in the position, whether on the basis of sex, race, ethnicity, training, or any other dimension, are more "risky" and that a greater burden of proof is necessary to demonstrate their competence or fit for the position.[21] Holding evaluators to high standards of accountability for the fairness of their evaluation, however, reduces the influence of bias and assumptions.[22]

Logistics for Managing the Review of Applicants

To conduct a fair and thorough review of applications, plan to break the review down into several stages:

1. **Selecting applicants who meet minimum qualification standards**
2. **Creating the "long short list" of applicants to consider further**
3. **Selecting a "short list" of finalists to interview**
4. **Evaluating the finalists**

Note: Some search committees will select the "short list" of finalists based solely on their review of application materials. Others, after their initial review of applicant materials, will interview applicants by telephone or at academic conferences before identifying their "short list." Advice for conducting interviews of all types is provided in Element V, pp. 73-102.

STAGE 1: Selecting applicants who meet minimum qualifications

Every set of applications for a given position will include at least some applicants who clearly do not meet qualifications—they do not have the required educational background, they lack the requisite minimum years of experience, or their field of expertise does not match areas identified in the job announcement. Ideally, all search committee members should briefly review application materials to determine whether applicants meet the minimum qualifications for the position. If this is not possible given the size of the committee and the number of applications, then each committee member can be responsible for reviewing a certain number of

---

21. Monica Biernat and Kathleen Fuegen, "Shifting Standards and the Evaluation of Competence: Complexity in Gender-Based Judgment and Decision Making," *Journal of Social Issues* 57;4 (2001): 707-724.

22. Michael Dobbs and William D. Crano, "Outgroup Accountability in the Minimal Group Paradigm: Implications for Aversive Discrimination and Social Identity Theory." *Personality and Social Psychology Bulletin* 27;3 (2001): 355-364; Martha Foschi, "Double Standards in the Evaluation of Men and Women," *Social Psychology Quarterly* 59;3 (1996): 237-254.

applications and each application should receive a review from at least two committee members. This task can be simplified and expedited by including a checklist of requirements in each applicant's folder (see Sample Form A, p. 62), and/or by maintaining a master checklist for all applicants (see Sample Form B, p. 63). An administrative assistant to the search committee or designated members of the committee can complete these forms prior to the committee's brief review. To ensure active involvement of search committee members, instill accountability, and provide a record of search committee deliberations, include a sign-in sheet (hard copy or electronic copy) in each applicant's folder. Committee members can use this sign-in sheet to confirm that they have conducted a brief evaluation and to record their assessment of whether or not the applicant meets qualifications (see Sample Form C, p. 64).

Generally, search committee members will readily reach consensus about which applicants are or are not qualified for the position. The challenge, at this stage of the evaluation, is for search committee members to avoid considering criteria or preferences not specified in the job announcement and to refrain from comparing applicants and developing preferences. **The goal is merely to assess which applicants meet the qualifications specified in the job announcement.** The search committee chair should review all applicants rejected at this stage in order to ensure that qualified applicants are not inadvertently rejected.

All applicants, regardless of whether they are qualified or not, should receive written confirmation that their application was received and, at designated points in the evaluation process, information about the status of their application. A checklist for communicating with applicants (Sample Form D) is included on p. 65, and sample letters for communicating with applicants are available on pp. 69-71 of this guidebook.

STAGE 2: Creating the "long short list" of applicants to consider further

During this stage, the committee's goal is to focus on identifying **all potentially interesting applicants**—to develop a "long short list" of potential applicants worthy of further consideration, not just a list of those regarded as "top candidates." If you have a large pool of applicants, it may be difficult for all members of the search committee to conduct a thorough review of all the applicants. In such situations, responsibilities for the review can be allocated as follows:

- All members of the committee should be responsible for conducting a brief review of all applications to gain a sense of the possibilities present in the pool. *(To ensure that each applicant is adequately reviewed, some search committee chairs recommend including a sign-in sheet, hard copy or electronic copy, in each applicant's file. Reviewers can use this form to indicate that they have briefly reviewed the file. See Sample Form E, p. 66.)*

- Responsibility for thoroughly evaluating the qualifications of each applicant can be divided equitably amongst the search committee in a manner consistent with the size of the committee and the pool of applicants. In assigning responsibilities for in-depth reviews of applicants, make sure that each applicant receives a thorough review from at least two, and preferably more, members of the committee, and that each committee member is responsible for thoroughly evaluating the qualifications of a manageable group of applicants. *(Again, to ensure that each applicant receives an adequate review, search committee members can use the sign-in form referred to above to indicate that they have completed a thorough review. See Sample Form E, p. 66. Some search committees provide a customized evaluation form that their members can use to keep track of their evaluations, while others prefer to let committee members devise their own methods for evaluating and comparing applicants. See Sample Form F, p. 67.)*

In conducting thorough reviews, keep the following advice in mind:

- Recognize that reading and thoroughly evaluating applicants' files will take considerable time. Set sufficient time aside for this task in your schedule. Inexperienced or busy committee members run the risk of putting off reading the files until it is too late to do a thorough evaluation. Recall the advice presented above about devoting your undivided attention to the review, which may take **at least 15–20 minutes per applicant**.

- Remember to concentrate on selecting **all potentially strong applicants** in the group you are reviewing—not just applicants you personally may prefer. In cases of doubt, retain applicants for further review by the entire committee.

- Make decisions using a process of inclusion (who should be included for further review) rather than exclusion (who should be rejected from consideration). Recall the study discussed above demonstrating that exclusion decision-making strategies not only resulted in larger pools of candidates, but were also more subject to the influence of bias and assumptions.

At a subsequent meeting (scheduled to allow sufficient time for search committee members to have completed their evaluations) decide how long the "long short list" should be and begin constructing the "long short list" by having the reviewers present their conclusions. It may be helpful to review the ground rules that the committee previously established, especially with regard to methods for making decisions (by consensus, by majority vote, etc.). As the committee discusses the applicants and begins to compile the "long short list," keep the following advice in mind:

- Rely on your previously established evaluation criteria to guide decisions.

- Focus discussion on whom to include, rather than whom to exclude.

- Pay particular attention to applicants on whom the designated reviewers disagree. Consider retaining such applicants in the "long short list" so that the entire committee has the opportunity to conduct a thorough review of their applications.

- Evaluate your "long short list" before finalizing it. Are qualified women and underrepresented applicants included? If not, consider whether evaluation biases or assumptions have influenced your ratings.

- Conduct the selection of the "short list" of candidates for interviews at a later meeting scheduled to allow committee members sufficient time to review thoroughly the strengths of the applicants on the "long short list."

STAGE 3: Selecting a "short list" of finalists to interview

This is likely to be the most difficult part of the review process, since committee members will inevitably have different perspectives or preferences with respect to the open position. Search committee chairs and members should think of ways to handle the potentially divisive issues that may arise. Some search committees will interview applicants on the "long-short list" by telephone, teleconference, online video chats, and/or at academic conferences before selecting the "short list" of finalists they invite to interview on-campus. Others will select final candidates for on-campus interviews based solely on their review of applicants included on their "long-short list." Whether they use preliminary interviews or not, many successful search committee chairs recommend the following:

To get the review off to a good start, with the entire committee willing to consider all applicants objectively:

- Review your objectives, criteria, procedures, and ground rules.

- Emphasize that the committee represents the interests of the department as a whole and, in a broader context, the interests of the entire university.

- Remember that your dean, department chair, and faculty colleagues will expect the search committee or its chair to make a convincing case that the review was complete and equitable. Some committee members may otherwise want to start by reviewing only their favorite applicants, and may dismiss consideration of other applicants without giving them a fair and thorough review.

To make sure that diversity is considered seriously:

- Before beginning the review of applicants, remind committee members of the potential role inadvertent biases or assumptions can play in evaluation. If necessary, review the brochure, *Reviewing Applicants: Research on Bias and Assumptions*.

- Insist upon the uniform application of standards in retaining or dropping applicants on the "long short list."

- Expect each search committee member to justify their advocacy for accepting or rejecting an applicant and ensure that they base this justification on criteria established for the position and evidence within the applicant's record.

- Remind the committee that increasing the diversity of the faculty is an important criterion to consider in choosing among otherwise comparable applicants.

To handle the mechanics of selecting the "short list' efficiently, systematically, and equitably:

- Have all members of the search committee thoroughly review and evaluate the applications of those selected for the "long short list" and remind them to devote at least 15–20 minutes to each application. *(See Sample Form F, p. 67.)*

- When scheduling subsequent committee meetings, take into account the time it will require for search committee members to conduct thorough evaluations.

- Decide on the "short list" and possible alternates only after the entire committee has had a chance to review the "long short list" in depth.

- Do not allow individuals or factions of the committee to dominate the process or to push for dropping or retaining applicants without defending their reasons. *(See Element I, p. 12).*

- Ensure that all committee members have an opportunity to share their opinions. *(See Element I, p. 13 for advice on eliciting views of quieter committee members.)*

- Do not allow personal preferences or narrow perspectives to dominate the process. Focus instead on the criteria established for the position and on the needs of the department and the school or college.

- Avoid relying on information not included in the application materials you requested. This includes information received from colleagues (e.g., rumors or innuendos about how well an applicant gets along with colleagues) as well as public knowledge about an applicant's personal life that should not be part of the evaluation (e.g., he or she is married, has children, is of a certain religious faith or sexual orientation, and more). Increasingly, search committees are tempted to rely on internet searches and social media to learn more about applicants than is revealed in their application materials. Despite the fact that the information available online is public, experts recommend exercising great caution.[23] If a search committee conducts such an investigation it should do so for all applicants. Its members should carefully consider what they expect to find that can't be revealed by the review of application materials and interviews with applicants. They should consciously avoid being influenced by information they might discover that is not related to applicants' qualifications for the position—especially if the information reveals aspects of applicants' identities that are protected by federal and state equal opportunity laws (e.g., sex, race, ethnicity, age, marital status, religious affiliation, sexual orientation, disabilities, and more).

- Evaluate each applicant's entire application. Do not depend too heavily on only one element such as the letters of recommendation, or the prestige of the degree-granting institution or postdoctoral program.

- Consider evaluating applicants on several different rating scales—one for teaching ability, one for research productivity, and one for mentoring experience or other factors. Determine the relative importance of different criteria.

- Consider including the top applicants from various different rating scales in the "short list."

- After search committee members present initial evaluations, review the ratings a second time. Opinions expressed early in the process can change after many applicants are considered and comparisons become more clear.

- Be sure that standards are being applied uniformly. **Be able to defend every decision for rejecting or retaining an applicant.**

- Evaluate your "short list" before finalizing it. Are qualified women and underrepresented minority applicants included? If not, consider whether evaluation biases or assumptions may be influencing your ratings.

- Keep sufficiently detailed notes so that the reasons for decisions will still be clear later.

- Resist the temptation to rank order the finalists on your "short list." Of necessity, the review process is based on incomplete information and on judgments about applicants' qualifications and potential that may or may not be accurate. Indeed, one goal of conducting on-campus interviews is to assess the extent to which candidates match the expectations you developed on the basis of their application materials. Ranking the final candidates before they visit may inadvertently influence your interactions with them. Instead, remind yourself that each candidate who has reached this stage of the process is highly qualified for the position, and strive to view the on-campus interviews with finalists as a fresh chance to evaluate and re-evaluate the candidates.

---

23. Courtney Hunt, "Social Screening: Candidates – and Employers – Beware," *Social Media in Organizations Community,* October 15, 2010, www.sminorgs.net/2010/10/social-screening-candidates-and -employers-beware.html, accessed April 18, 2012.

STAGE 4: Evaluating the finalists

The search committee should meet right after each candidate's visit to assess the candidate's strengths and weaknesses. If it is not possible for the committee to meet after each visit, then search committee members should take notes immediately after each visit to record their personal assessments of each candidate. Similarly, any feedback sought from other groups or individuals with whom the candidate met should be collected as soon after the candidate's visit as possible. It is important to collect feedback and record assessments in a timely manner because evaluators may forget aspects of the first candidate's visit by the time the last candidate's visit is over, or may confuse their impressions of one candidate with those of another. Indeed, research indicates a wide variety of factors differentially influence our memory of behaviors and personalities that are consistent or inconsistent with common stereotypes. Selective recall of stereotype consistent or inconsistent information can influence evaluation of candidates but can be avoided by promptly recording and conducting assessments and evaluations.[24] *(Some search committees provide forms that search committee members and others with whom the candidates meet can use to record their assessments and observations. See Sample Form G, p. 68.)*

Before evaluating final candidates, the search committee should review the advice on minimizing bias presented earlier in this chapter and should take the time to consider their objectives, evaluation criteria, and ground rules once more. This will be the committee's last opportunity to ensure that the evaluation process is fair and equitable.

---

24. Stangor, Charles and David McMillan, "Memory for Expectancy-Congruent and Expectancy-Incongruent Information: A Review of the Social and Social Developmental Literatures," *Psychological Bulletin* 111;1 (1992): 42-61.

RESOURCES

Sample forms to help keep track of and communicate with applicants

Please note that the forms on the following pages are intended only as samples.

You may choose to use, modify, or ignore these forms according to your needs or preferences.

These forms were adapted from the following sources:

Dean Pribbenow, *Improving the interview and selection process* (Madison, WI: UW-Madison Office of Quality Improvement, 2002).

Estela Mara Bensimon, Kelly Ward, and Karla Sanders, *The Department Chair's Role in Developing New Faculty into Teachers and Scholars* (Bolton, MA: Ankar Publishing Co., 2000).

RESOURCES

Sample Form A

Checklist: Application materials for individual applicants

Some search committee chairs recommend including a form such as this one in a folder (electronic or hard copy) created for each applicant. Most search chairs recommend that a single form to track the application materials for all applicants supplement or replace this form for individual applicants.

Please note that this form is intended as a sample only.
You may choose to use, modify, or ignore it according to your needs.

Applicant name _____

Evaluator/s _____

The applicant has submitted the following materials by the due date:

Cover letter addressing qualifications _____

Curriculum vitae/résumé _____

Description of research program/interests _____

Statement of teaching interests/teaching philosophy _____

Sample/s of scholarly work _____

Three letters of reference _____

University transcripts _____

Other _____

Sample Form B

Checklist: Application materials for ALL applicants

Please note that this form is intended as a sample only.
You may choose to use, modify, or ignore it according to your needs.

Applicant Name	Cover letter addressing qualifications	Curriculum vitae or résumé	Description of research interests	Statement of teaching interests	Samples of scholarly work	3 Letters of Reference	University Transcripts	Other

RESOURCES

Sample Form C

Sign-in sheet for preliminary evaluation of qualifications

Search committee chairs who use this type of form recommend keeping one in each applicant's folder (electronic or hard copy).

Please note that this form is intended as a sample only.
You may choose to use, modify, or ignore it according to your needs.

Applicant's name _____

Search Committee Member's Name	Assessment of Qualifications Signature and Date	Meets Minimum Qualifications (Yes/No)				
		Degree	Relevant Field of Research	Teaching Experience	Publication Record	Other

Ideally, all search committee members should briefly review each application to determine if the applicant meets all minimal qualifications for the position. If this is not possible given the size of the committee and the number of applications, then at least two committee members (and preferably more) should review each application.

RESOURCES

Sample Form D

Checklist for communicating with applicants

Please note that this form is intended as a sample only.
You may choose to use, modify, or ignore it according to your needs.

Applicant name	Date application received	Date letter of receipt sent	Decision on Status			Date letter of status sent	Interview scheduled	Final decision		Date letter of final decision sent
			Not qualified	Qualified but not selected as finalist	Selected as finalist			Hire	Don't hire	

Sample letters for communicating with applicants regarding the receipt and status of their application are available on pp. 69-71 of this guidebook.

RESOURCES

Sample Form E

Sign-in sheet for evaluation of applicants

Search committee chairs who use this type of form recommend keeping one in each applicant's folder (electronic or hard copy).

**Please note that this form is intended as a sample only.
You may choose to use, modify, or ignore it according to your needs.**

Applicant's Name _____			
Search Committee Member's Name	Brief Evaluation (for long short list) Signature and Date	Complete Evaluation (for long short list) Signature and Date	Complete Evaluation (for short list) Signature and Date

For developing the "long short list," at least two search committee members should perform a thorough and complete evaluation of each applicant.

In order to create the "short list," every committee member should conduct a thorough evaluation of each applicant on the "long short list."

RESOURCES

Sample Form F

Evaluation of faculty applicants

**Please note that this form is intended as a sample only.
You may choose to use, modify, or ignore it according to your needs.**

CAUTION: If your institution is subject to Public Records laws and completed forms such as this are shared publicly in search committee meetings, they may become part of the official record and may be subject to disclosure should someone file an Open Records request. If individual search committee members use or adapt a form such as this as a means of taking private notes to remind them of their evaluation of each applicant and do not share the document publicly, it may not become part of the public record.

Applicant's Name _____

Reviewer's Name (If form is shared in committee)_____

I = Inadequate; A = Adequate; G = Good; E = Excellent

	I	A	G	E
Educational background or PhD in relevant area of study				
Postdoctoral experience				
Teaching experience				
Research experience				
Creativity or innovation of research				
Publication history				
Service contributions				
Experience working with or teaching diverse groups including women and members of underrepresented minority groups				
Meets departmental needs				
Recommendation letters				

Particular strengths this applicant offers:

Concerns this applicant presents:

RESOURCES

Sample Form G

Review of final candidates - Feedback

**Please note that this form is intended as a sample only.
You may choose to use, modify, or ignore it according to your needs.**

Reviewer's Name _____

Candidate's Name _____

I = Inadequate; A = Adequate; G = Good; E = Excellent; n/a = did not attend

	I	A	G	E	n/a
Reviewed candidate's cover letter and curriculum vitae/resume					
Read candidate's research/teaching statement/philosophy					
Read candidate's scholarship/selected publications					
Read candidate's letters of recommendation					
Met individually with candidate					
Attended a group meeting with candidate					
Attended candidate's research presentation					
Observed candidate's teaching demonstration, or Attended discussion regarding teaching/pedagogy					
Attended a meal with candidate					
Spoke with candidate at a reception					
Other (specify)					

Particular strengths this candidate offers:

Concerns this candidate presents:

Note: This form is adapted from the University of Michigan ADVANCE Candidate Evaluation Tool, www.umich.edu/%7Eadvproj/CandidateEvaluationTool.doc, accessed 7/18/2012.

RESOURCES

Sample Letters to Applicants

Adapted from the University of Wisconsin–Madison Office of Human Resources, "Recruitment Toolkit"
http://go.wisc.edu/48k0f1

Acknowledging receipt of application materials

Name of Applicant
Address
City, State, Zipcode

Dear (Name):

This is to acknowledge receipt of your application for the position of (Name of Position) in the (Name of the Department, College, or Division) at the (Name of Institution). We are currently reviewing applications and expect to schedule interviews in the next couple of weeks. I will notify you of your status after the initial screening of applications.

(Include any relevant policy statements. For example, a confidentiality statement: Please note that unless confidentiality is requested in writing, information regarding applicants must be released upon request. Finalists cannot be guaranteed confidentiality.)

Thank you for your interest in the position. We appreciate the time you invested in this application.

Sincerely,

(Name), Chair
(Position) Search Committee

Response to applications received after the deadline

Name of Applicant
Address
City, State, Zipcode

Dear (Name):

Thank you for your interest in the position of (Name of Position) in the (Name of Department), (Name of Institution). Because your application was received after the deadline, I regret to inform you that we are no longer accepting applications. If the position is announced again in the future, I encourage you to reapply at that time.

Best wishes for a successful job search.

Sincerely,

(Name), Chair
(Position) Search Committee

RESOURCES

Response to applicants who DO NOT meet minimum qualifications

Name of Applicant
Address
City, State, Zipcode

Dear (Name):

We have completed the initial screening of applications for the position of (Name of Postion) in the (Name of Department) at the (Name of Institution). I am sorry to inform you that you do not meet the minimum qualifications for the position.

Thank you for your interest in employment with us. I wish you success in your job search.

Sincerely,

(Name), Chair
(Position) Search Committee

Response to qualified applicants not selected to interview for the position

Name of Applicant
Address
City, State, Zipcode

Dear (Name):

The Search Committee for the position of (Name of Position) in the (Name of Department) at the (Name of Institution) has met to review the credentials of the applicants. The Committee has studied your application with great care. Nonetheless, the Committee has judged that your background and experience does not correspond fully to the University's needs at the present time.

We appreciate your interest in (Name of Institution) and wish you well in your profes-sional and career development.

Sincerely,

(Name), Chair
(Position) Search Committee

RESOURCES

Invitation to qualified applicants to interview on campus

Name of Applicant
Address
City, State, Zipcode

Dear (Name):

I am pleased to inform you that you have been selected as a finalist to interview for the position of (Name of Position) in the (Name of Department) at the (Name of Institution). We will be in communication with you regarding the date and travel arrangements for your on-campus interview.

(Include any relevant policy statements. For example, a statement on accommodations: It is the policy of the (Name of Institution) to provide reasonable accommodations for qualified persons with disabilities who are employees or applicants for employment. If you need assistance or accommodations to interview because of a disability, please contact (Name) at (contact information). Employment opportunities will not be denied to anyone because of the need to make reasonable accommodations to a person's disability.)

I look forward to meeting with you.

Sincerely,

(Name), Chair
(Position) Search Committee

Response to qualified finalists not selected (at end of search)

Name of Applicant
Address
City, State, Zipcode

Dear (Name):

Thank you very much for interviewing for the position of (Name of Position) in the (Name of Department) at the (Name of Institution). I am sorry to inform you that the position has been offered to and accepted by another applicant.

Thank you for your interest in this position. We wish you success in your job search.

Sincerely,

(Name), Chair
(Position) Search Committee

V. DEVELOP AND IMPLEMENT AN EFFECTIVE INTERVIEW PROCESS

Key aims of the interview (p. 74)

BEFORE: Planning for an effective interview process (pp. 74–87)

All interview types
Telephone interviews
Videoconference or online video interviews
Interviews at academic conferences
On-campus interviews

DURING: Guidelines for interviewing (pp. 87–90)

Interviews by telephone, videoconference or online video,
and at academic conferences
On-campus interviews

AFTER: Evaluating the interviewed candidates (pp. 90–91)

Interviews by telephone, videoconference or online video,
and at academic conferences
On-campus interviews

Resources (pp. 93–102)

Advice for interviewing
Video conferencing etiquette
Sample interview questions
Appropriate and inappropriate interview questions
Tips for interviewing applicants with disabilities
Materials to include in an informational packet
Sample letter to include in an informational packet

Key Aims of the Interview

Once a search committee has identified applicants for further consideration, it is time to begin planning for interviews. Some search committees will select final candidates for on-campus interviews based solely on their review of applicants on their "long-short list." Others will interview applicants on the "long-short list" by telephone, teleconference, videoconference or online video calling (e.g., Skype or Google Chat), and/or at academic conferences before selecting the "short list" of finalists they invite to interview on-campus.

For all types of interviews, it is important to keep in mind the dual nature of the interview process:

- Interviews allow hiring departments to determine whether candidates possess the knowledge, skills, abilities, and other attributes required for the position, and

- Interviews allow candidates to assess whether the hiring department and the institution offer opportunities, facilities, colleagues, and other factors that meet their personal and professional needs.

To ensure an effective interview process and to enhance the quality of the overall hiring process, keep **both of these aims** in mind as you plan what to do before, during, and after the actual interviews.

Before: Planning for an Effective Interview Process

Planning: All interview types

1. **Together with your committee, articulate your interview goals**
   Review and reflect on the desired qualifications of candidates. Ensure that the interview process you design will provide you with sufficient information to make your decisions.

2. **Develop a set of core questions to ask all candidates**
   Plan to spend time on developing a set of questions to ask of all candidates. These questions should pertain to the evaluation criteria you previously developed and should elicit complex answers rather than simple yes or no responses (see "Sample Interview Questions," pp. 95-97). The questions should also aim to supplement information already provided in the application materials. Build sufficient flexibility into your interview structure to allow for unscripted follow-up questions based on the responses you receive.

   Although some search committee chairs prefer to rely on unstructured interviews rather than on a prepared set of questions, research demonstrates that structured interviews provide more equitable evaluations of candidates than do unstructured interviews. Structured interviews also ensure that someone asks each candidate the questions that are critical to your evaluation and comparison of all candidates.[1]

---

1. Nora P. Reilly, Shawn P. Bocketti, Stephen A. Maser, and Craig L. Wennet, "Benchmarks Affect Perceptions of Prior Disability in a Structured Interview," *Journal of Business and Psychology* 20;4 (2006): 489-500; Eugene J. Kutcher and Jennifer DeNicolis Bragger, "Selection Interviews of Overweight Job Applicants: Can Structure Reduce the Bias?" *Journal of Applied Social Psychology* 34;10 (2004): 1993-2022; Jennifer DeNicolis Bragger, Eugene Kutcher, John Morgan, and Patricia Firth, "The Effects of the

Whether structured or informal, interview questions might include those relating to the following areas:

- Educational background
- Research experience
- Teaching experience
- Publication record
- Vision for the position
- Current and future research interests
- Current funding and potential sources of future funding
- Ideas for future publications
- Experience teaching and/or mentoring women and members of minority groups
- Ideas for fostering excellence and diversity in the discipline, department, and/or profession

Despite your efforts to ask each candidate all the questions you believe will be relevant to your evaluation, committee members may find themselves evaluating one candidate on the basis of a response to an issue not raised with the remaining candidates. In such cases, consider conducting follow-up telephone conversations with the remaining candidates to solicit their responses and provide your committee with the ability to make comparisons.

3. **Be sure all interviewers are aware of what questions are inappropriate**
   Inappropriate questions are those that elicit personal information from candidates that have nothing to do with their abilities to perform the job. Asking such questions can not only introduce bias into the evaluation of candidates, but can make your institution vulnerable to a lawsuit if a candidate not hired believes that his or her responses to such questions influenced the hiring decision. Because such lawsuits rely on federal laws prohibiting discrimination based on race, color, religion, sex, national origin, disability, or age, and on state laws preventing discrimination against additional categories (sexual orientation, marital status, conviction record, and more), it is important to avoid asking your candidates questions related to their personal lives. See pp. 98-99 for a list of inappropriate questions.

4. **Prepare for the possibility of evaluating internal candidates**
   Develop procedures for ensuring that you provide internal candidates with the same treatment as external candidates. To do so, some committees recommended conducting phone interviews, videoconference interviews, or interviews at conferences with internal candidates if you do so for external candidates. For on-campus interviews, they recommend interviewing internal candidates before interviewing external candidates. This policy fosters equity by ensuring that the interview responses and presentations of internal candidates are not influenced by their ability to observe the presentations of and reactions to external candidates. Finally, if you host social events or dinners for external candidates, you should also do so for internal candidates.

Structured Interview on Reducing Biases Against Pregnant Job Applicants," *Sex Roles* 46;7/8 (2002): 215-226.

5. Develop plans for evaluating candidates during and after the interview

See Element IV for advice on fairly evaluating candidates. The advice provided for Stages 3 and 4 of the evaluation process is particularly relevant (pp. 56-59).

Planning: Telephone interviews

1. Develop an agenda for the conversation

Telephone interviews typically range from 30 to 45 minutes in length. Because of this short timeframe, it is helpful to develop an agenda for the interview. Decide in advance how much time to devote to introductions, to questions relating to the applicant's research, to questions about teaching, and to questions about other areas relevant to your search. Be sure to allot some time for the applicant to ask questions of the interviewer/s.

2. Designate a timekeeper

It will be very helpful to designate one member of the committee or the interview team as a timekeeper who will signal the interviewer/s when it is time to move on to the next topic. Failing to do so may prevent some applicants from addressing all of the committee's questions. This will limit the committee's ability to make meaningful comparisons between interviewed applicants.

3. Determine who will conduct and participate in the interview

Some committees prefer to designate one member as the interviewer—the person asking all the questions. One advantage of doing so is that the interviewee will always know who is speaking and will not be confronted with multiple disembodied voices. Other committees may assign specific search members to ask designated questions or may simply have members take turns asking questions. If more than one committee member asks questions during the interview, each member should plan to introduce or identify him- or herself before speaking.

Committees should also determine in advance whether they will encourage members other than those designated to ask specific questions to participate in the interview by interjecting with follow-up questions. Discouraging such participation will ease the task of managing the timing of the interview but may also result in a rather stilted conversation. Encouraging follow-up questions may enrich the conversation and enhance the committee's ability to evaluate the applicant. As recommended above, committee members should identify or introduce themselves before asking follow-up questions.

If a search committee does choose to designate only one person to be responsible for asking all the questions, it is especially important for other members of the committee to participate in the interview by listening to the conversation, making their own individual assessments about the applicant's merits, and subsequently sharing their assessments with the entire committee. If a committee plans to record an interview for members with scheduling conflicts, the applicant being interviewed should be informed in advance. In some cases, state laws require that all parties to a recorded telephone conversation consent to the recording. If you are calling someone in a state that requires such consent you may be subject to that state's laws. For more information and a list of states requiring consent from all parties see: www.citmedialaw.org/legal-guide/recording-phone-calls-and-conversations.

4. Maximize audio quality with appropriate telephone equipment and use

- If the search committee plans to gather in one room to participate jointly in the telephone interview, use a special teleconference phone with multiple speakers and microphones. This equipment will provide far better audio quality than will a standard telephone with a "speaker phone" function. Even if **you** can hear the applicant you are interviewing using a "speaker phone," **the applicant may have great difficulty hearing the search committee members** who may be sitting at various distances from the phone. Investigate whether media services, instructional technology, or information technology offices in your school, college, or institution loan teleconference equipment to faculty and staff.

- If you plan to use a teleconference service that enables search committee members to dial into the conference from their own phones, encourage committee members to use landlines rather than cellular phones and to minimize ambient noise by muting their phones when they are not speaking. Many phones have a mute button or can be muted by pressing *6.

5. **Clearly communicate relevant phone call details in advance**

- **Clarify who will initiate the phone call.** In most cases, the search committee should initiate the call, ensuring that the applicant is not responsible for the cost of a lengthy long-distance telephone call.

- **When scheduling calls, remind participants about differences in time zones and/or daylight savings time.** Examples abound of search committee members and applicants who made or received calls earlier or later than expected due to confusion or miscalculations involving time zones or daylight savings time. You can reduce frustration and conduct more effective interviews by double checking these details with all parties involved and by ensuring that everyone knows what time the call will take place in their own time zone.

- **Provide information to the applicant** about who will participate in the call and how long it will last. If any details change before the call occurs, inform the applicant of the changes. This allows applicants to prepare adequately for the call.

6. **Recognize that applicants with hearing or other disabilities may be unable to participate effectively in a standard telephone interview**
Be prepared to accommodate the needs of applicants who have hearing or other disabilities. This may involve using a phone relay service, TTY device, or other accommodations requested by an applicant. Committee members should be careful about not allowing an applicant's need for accommodations to bias their evaluation.

Planning: Videoconference or online video interviews

Increasingly, search committees are replacing telephone or conference interviews with videoconferences or online video interviews (e.g., interviews conducted using Skype, Google's video chat, Adobe Connect, and similar services). Much of the advice presented above for phone interviews applies to videoconference or online video interviews. Please review the sections on:

- Develop an agenda
- Designate a time keeper
- Determine who will conduct and participate in the interview
- Clearly communicate relevant details about the interview including its time and length

Additional advice pertains largely to issues relating to the technology used for the interview.

1. **Maximize audio and video quality by using appropriate equipment or software**
Recognize that many free online video services (e.g., Skype or Google's video chat) are designed to facilitate audio and video communication between two people, each relying on

their own computer's web camera, microphone, and speakers. Gathering several people around one computer to interview an applicant has disadvantages similar to gathering around a speaker phone—you may hear and possibly see the applicant well, but the applicant may have difficulty seeing and hearing all members of your group, which will diminish the effectiveness of the interview. Better alternatives may include using "group video calling" services (such as Google Hangouts or Skype Premium) or investigating whether other video-conferencing software (such as Adobe Connect or Blackboard Collaborate) are available through your school, college, or campus. These alternatives enable individual members of the committee to join the videoconference from their own computers.

2. **Recognize that not all applicants have access to the technology needed to participate in a videoconference**

    Avoid making the assumption that because a computer is the only equipment needed, everyone will be equally able to participate in a videoconference. The computer used by the applicant must be equipped with a web camera and must have sufficient power and speed to handle the video and audio feeds. In addition, the internet service to which the computer connects must provide sufficient bandwidth and speed to transmit audio and video. Not all applicants will own or have access to computers and internet services that meet these needs. While some may argue that applicants who do not own adequate technology can always rely on resources provided by their academic institution, it is important to recognize that it may not always be appropriate to rely on these resources. For example, applicants who have not yet informed their current employer that they are searching for a new position may not want to conduct an interview at their place of work or use institutional resources for that search.

    In such cases, the search committee should be willing to make arrangements that will enable applicants to participate effectively in the interview process. This may include conducting a telephone interview instead of a video conference or covering applicants' costs for purchasing a web camera, renting an appropriate computer, or utilizing a video conference room and services provided by a local business.

    It is particularly important for a search committee to acknowledge that an applicant's access to the necessary technological resources is not relevant to his or her qualifications for the position. Committee members should be careful about not allowing bias regarding an applicant's lack of access to technological resources to influence their evaluation.

3. **Recognize that some applicants with visual, hearing, or other disabilities may not be able to participate effectively in a video conference**

    Be prepared to accommodate the needs of applicants who have visual, hearing or other disabilities. This may involve using a telephone interview, a phone relay service, a TTY device, or other accommodations requested by an applicant. Committee members should avoid allowing an applicant's need for accommodations to bias their evaluation.

4. **Be prepared to handle technical difficulties**

    If possible, test all equipment and connections prior to conducting the interview. Be sure to have contact information for technical support staff with you and check that they can be available to assist you if necessary. Consider having a telephone or teleconferencing equipment available as a backup in case you encounter technical difficulties.

Planning: Interviews at academic conferences

Conducting interviews at academic conferences is common in many disciplines, particularly those in the humanities, business, and law. This practice takes advantage of the fact that many scholars from a particular discipline will be in the same place at the same time. The conference thus provides a relatively convenient opportunity for job seekers and job providers to connect. Though convenient, interviewing at academic conferences also poses several challenges. These challenges and advice for conducting interviews at academic conferences are discussed below.

1. **Determine who will conduct the interviews**

   Search committees planning to conduct interviews at academic conferences will need to determine which of their members will attend the conference and devote time to conducting interviews. Because different members will likely bring varied perspectives to the evaluation of applicants, the committee should plan to send a team of interviewers to the conference rather than relying on interviews and evaluations conducted by any lone member of the committee. If the interview team includes department members not serving on the search committee, share the committee's expectations and evaluation criteria with them and ask them to prepare for the interviews by thoroughly reading the application materials submitted by each interviewee.

   If a department, school, college, or university cannot afford to send a team of interviewers to the academic conference, the committee should consider relying on telephone or video-conference interviews instead.

2. **Location of the interview sessions**

   Because multiple institutions and applicants are interviewing in the same place over a short period of time, finding appropriate places for interviewing can pose problems. Some commonly used options—"job or interview centers," hotel rooms, and other public spaces—are discussed below:

   - **Job/interview centers:** Some academic organizations establish "job centers" in the conference hotel where interviewers can reserve private or semi-private rooms or tables for conducting interviews. Despite this effort to provide an official space for interviewing, there may not always be enough rooms or tables to accommodate all interviewers, so other alternatives are necessary. In addition, some institutions or departments prefer not to use the job centers. Some may simply be choosing to save money because there may be a fee for using interview rooms or tables. Others, however, avoid using the job center because they dislike the lack of privacy that accompanies interviewing in the job center. Interviewers and job applicants can usually see (and sometimes, hear) who is being interviewed for which positions. Many institutions consequently prefer other spaces for interviews.

   - **Hotel rooms:** Conducting interviews in a hotel room is a common, though frequently discouraged, alternative. Academic organizations that discourage this practice do so because the setting is decidedly unprofessional and has the potential for creating significant discomfort for many applicants.[2] Indeed, applicants who feel uneasy in this environment are not likely to perform to the best of their abilities. If you must use a hotel room, a suite with a seating area separate from the bedroom is preferable and the interviewing team should include at least one man and one woman. The American Historical Association

---

2. See for example: David Darlington, "AHA Today: The Job Center: What Candidates Need to Know," American Historical Association Annual Meeting, November 23, 2010, http://blog.historians.org /annual-meeting/1184/the-job-center-what-candidates-need-to-know, accessed 2/15/2012 and "Chronicle Forums: Interviewing in a Hotel Room?" *Chronicle of Higher Education,* November 2007, http://chronicle.com/forums/index.php/topic,43921.0.html, accessed 2/15/2012.

provides additional advice for search committees who do not heed their recommendation to avoid using hotel rooms. This advice includes "providing proper seating [i.e. chairs, not beds] for all interviewers and candidates" and "asking the hotel's housekeeping department to clean the room before interviewing begins."[3]

- **Lobbies, restaurants, and other public spaces:** Though preferable to hotel rooms, other public spaces pose different challenges for conducting interviews. They share the same lack of privacy associated with "job centers" established by academic organizations, yet provide less control over the environment. Conducting interviews in such settings can result in interruptions by noisy clientele, waiters trying to do their jobs, or colleagues stopping by to say hello. Consumption of alcoholic beverages during the interview can also hamper interviewers' abilities to evaluate applicants effectively.

3. Consider how you will meet the needs of applicants with disabilities

Be aware that the ambient noise level in the "job center" and in many public places can pose difficulties for applicants with hearing impairments or attention deficit disorders. Narrow aisles or pathways and crowded conditions in all of the spaces discussed above can create barriers for applicants who rely on wheelchairs, other mobility devices, or service dogs.[4] Be prepared to make alternative arrangements if needed, or better yet, select a location that will meet the needs of all applicants.

4. Scheduling the interview sessions

In scheduling interviews, take into consideration the multiple goals members of the interview team may need to accomplish during the conference. They may need to attend presentations, give talks, serve on panels, participate in committee meetings, and network with colleagues. Develop a schedule that will allow interviewers to meet their obligations and objectives. This may be accomplished by not scheduling interviews at times when team members have conflicts, or by developing a system that allows interviewers to rotate on or off the team in such a way that a group of sufficient size is always present for the interviews.

Schedule sufficient time between interviews (10 to 15 minutes) to allow interviewers to take a brief break, to discuss and evaluate the applicant just interviewed, and to ensure that applicants do not run into each other, or worse, overhear the interview preceding them.

Understand that applicants may be juggling complicated interview schedules and try to make accommodations if they have other interviews or a presentation that conflicts with the time you selected.

5. Prepare your applicants for the interview

Provide your applicants with detailed information about when and where the interview will take place, how long it will take, and who will be participating in the interview. If you will not have detailed information about where the interview will occur until during the conference, provide the applicants with accurate information about how and when they can obtain this information.

---

3. American Historical Association, "AHA Guidelines for the Hiring Process," November 26, 2011, www.historians.org/Perspectives/eib/hiring_guidelines.htm, accessed 2/15/2012.

4. Sarah F. Rose, "Disability and the Academic Job Market," *Disability Studies Quarterly* 28;3 (2008). http://dsq-sds.org/article/view/111/111, accessed 2/17/2012.

6. **Don't assume all applicants can or will attend the annual meeting**
   Interviewing applicants at academic conferences presumes that anyone on the job market will be attending the conference to take advantage of networking opportunities and the possibility of interviewing for positions. It is also assumes that most departments conducting active job searches will send faculty representatives to the annual meeting to conduct interviews. Neither assumption is necessarily correct.

   Increasingly, departments are opting to reduce costs by not conducting interviews at annual conferences.[5] Traveling to a conference also places a heavy financial burden on job applicants, especially on recent or soon to be graduates who may be supporting themselves and possibly a family on a small stipend or salary. Many applicants may be reluctant to purchase non-refundable airfare to attend the conference without knowing that they have received an invitation to interview. Yet, if they wait for an invitation, they may lose the opportunity to purchase lower priced airfare or lodging.

   Search committees can help ease the inevitable stress associated with a job search by letting applicants know whether or not they plan to conduct interviews at an annual meeting and by striving to select and invite applicants to interview within a time frame that will provide them with the opportunity to purchase lower rate airfare.

   Search committee members should also understand that a variety of circumstances—financial hardship, family obligations, health issues, or employment obligations—may prevent an applicant from attending the conference. In such cases, and despite the goal of providing a similar experience for all interviewees, the search committee can provide the applicant with an alternative type of interview.

   The ability to attend the annual conference, in other words, should not become a qualification criterion for the position.

7. **Be prepared to handle complications caused by travel delays**
   Given the uncertainties associated with air travel—cancelled flights, weather-related delays, and more—develop a plan for handling situations in which applicants cannot make their scheduled interview. This might include attempting to reschedule interviews or arranging for an alternative type of interview after the conference concludes.

Planning: On-campus interviews

The advice provided at the beginning of this chapter, to keep in mind the dual nature of the interview process, is particularly relevant to on-campus interviews. During this type of interview, more so than during any other type, the search committee and department are not only evaluating candidates, but hosting them as well. One goal of every campus visit should be to ensure that every candidate, whether they are offered a position or not, has a good experience

---

5. Audrey Williams June, "Faculty Job Interviews Move from Scholarly Meetings to Campuses," *Chronicle of Higher Education*, May 2, 2010, http://chronicle.com/article/Faculty-Job-Interviews-Move/65336, accessed 2/16/2012; and The Young Philosopher, "End Conference Interviews," *Inside Higher Ed*, February 11, 2011, insidehighered.com/advice/2011/02/11/a_call_to_end_conference_interviews, accessed 2/16/2012.

during the visit and leaves with a positive impression of the department, school, college and/or university. Considerable advance planning is needed to achieve this goal.[6]

1. **Make and discuss travel arrangements in consultation with your candidates**

   - **For airfare:** Consult with your candidates about preferred airlines, dates, and times for travel. Be clear about who will be responsible for making reservations and paying the airfare. Having the hiring department make and pay for reservations prevents candidates from needing to use their own funds and await reimbursement. Yet, some candidates may prefer having the flexibility to make their own reservations. If your policies require candidates to pay for their own flights, or if any candidate prefers to make his or her own reservation, be sure to provide instructions about how to request reimbursement, information about the documents or receipts required, and an estimate of how long the process will take.

   - **For hotel accommodations:** As with airfare, the department can save candidates considerable trouble by making and paying for hotel accommodation rather than expecting candidates to cover the expense and wait for reimbursement. Choose a hotel that you know will be comfortable and that will maximize your candidates' chances for getting a good night's sleep before a full day of interviewing. Consider whether the hotel you choose has good internet service and access to printing services in case your candidates need to make use of them. Considering such factors may help you determine that a popular hotel conveniently located near campus or restaurants may not be ideal if it is also in an area known for being noisy late at night. Likewise, a delightful bed and breakfast in a quiet part of town with weak internet service or rooms reached only by climbing a rickety staircase may not meet your candidates' needs.

   - **Transportation to and from the airport:** Plan to have a member of the search committee meet and welcome candidates at the airport, drive them to their hotel or first appointment in a clean and reliable vehicle, and return them to the airport at the end of the event. If a candidate is arriving very late at night and it is not practical to provide a ride, arrange for a hotel shuttle, a taxicab, or a limousine service to provide transportation. Be sure to arrange for this in advance. In many airports, other than those located in major cities, shuttles and taxicabs do not routinely wait for passengers arriving late at night. If you do make such arrangements, let your candidate know exactly where to meet the shuttle or cab. Similarly, if the nearest airport is an hour or more out of town and it is not feasible to welcome candidates at the airport, make arrangements for their travel in advance. If the candidate will be using his or her own funds to pay for transportation, provide them with information about how to obtain reimbursement.

2. **Develop an agenda or schedule for the interview**
   Decide what events the candidates will engage in (e.g., an interview with the search committee, interviews with individuals and other groups, a research presentation, a classroom presentation, campus and community tours, meals, social events).

---

6. Some of the advice presented in this section is based on interview experiences shared with us by faculty participants in search workshops at the University of Wisconsin-Madison and at various other universities across the nation. We thank them for contributing to our knowledge of positive and negative interview experiences.

- For interviews, determine which individuals and/or groups will interview each candidate and confirm that they will actually be available to conduct the interviews on the day each candidate visits.

- For meals with the candidate, carefully consider the purpose of the meal and how many people to invite. If you expect to evaluate the candidate during the meal, a group of two to four members plus the candidate is most effective. If the purpose of the meal is primarily to provide the candidate with a chance to learn more about your department, campus, or community, a larger group might be more appropriate.

- Try to build some flexibility into candidates' schedules. Some search committees, for example, set aside a block of unscheduled time during which candidates can choose to meet with university personnel outside the search committee, department, school, or college and learn more about how university and community resources might meet their personal needs and interests.

3. **Personalize the visit for each candidate**
   In addition to selecting a core set of individuals or groups that all candidates will meet with, rely on each candidate's application materials to identify people with related research and teaching interests and include these individuals in relevant meetings, interviews, or events. Ask your candidates if there are any particular individuals or groups they would like to meet with.

4. **Provide opportunities for departmental faculty members who belong to underrepresented groups to meet all candidates**
   Avoid making the mistake of including faculty members from underrepresented groups in your schedule of events only when you know that the candidate is a woman or a member of an underrepresented minority group. You may not always know that a candidate belongs to a minority group. Events at which candidates can meet other faculty who share their sex, race, or ethnicity can help them feel welcome. Even candidates who belong to a majority group may want to see that the department is diverse, inclusive, and welcoming. Certainly, members of your department who belong to underrepresented groups will want to meet and be included in events for all faculty candidates, not just those with whom they share common identities. At the same time, ensure that you are not overburdening faculty members from underrepresented groups by expecting them to be more involved in the search process than are faculty from well-represented groups.

5. **Keep candidates' comfort and convenience in mind**
   As you plan your agenda or schedule of events, take into consideration the comfort and convenience of your candidates. Some suggestions for creating an environment that will allow each candidate to perform to the best of his or her ability are listed below:

- Allow sufficient time between meetings for traveling or walking to the next meeting, and for bathroom breaks.

- Always provide an escort to accompany the candidate from one meeting or event to the next.

- If you plan a lunch event that requires the candidate to answer questions and engage with attendees, build in some quiet time after the lunch for him or her to finish eating the meal.

- Offer candidates drinks of water throughout the day—they will be doing a lot of talking and may need the hydration.

- Provide candidates with a break before their main research presentation or job talk and with a comfortable space that will allow them to rest, gather their thoughts, or do some last minute preparation.

- Arrange for any necessary audio-visual and electronic equipment to be available in the room/s you have reserved. Make sure that you can operate this equipment successfully or that someone is available to provide technical assistance. Be sure to have contact information for technical support in hand on the day of the event in case any difficulties arise.

- If you plan to host a dinner for each candidate, allow your candidate to enjoy the meal by engaging all present in conversations and not continually asking questions of the candidate.

- Consider the comfort of your candidates especially at dinner or other large social events. If the candidate is a woman and no other women are present, will the candidate feel at ease? If the candidate will be the only person of a particular race or ethnicity, how will you ensure his or her comfort and feelings of safety? These kinds of social situations can be uncomfortable for persons in the minority and may lead them to lose interest in joining your department. Inviting people who share interests or identities with your candidates cannot not only help them feel comfortable but can also help them learn how they will fit into your department or community.

Consider developing a set of questions to ask of all candidates that will help you learn how best to meet their needs. These questions include those you would ask of any visiting speaker you may be hosting, but can also include questions that will allow you to incorporate principles of "universal design" into planning for your interviews. Though originally coined to refer to the design of buildings and spaces that accommodate the needs of people with a diverse range of abilities, "universal design," more broadly defined, refers to designing a process or event that will meet the needs of people with a diverse range of abilities without requiring them to ask for accommodations. Some recommendations include the following:

- Ask your candidates if they have any dietary restrictions and/or preferences and rely on their responses to guide your choice of restaurants, meals, and receptions.

- Ask your candidates if they have any specific transportation needs and if they would prefer to drive or walk between program events.

- If a tour of campus or of the community is included in the visit, ask your candidates if they would prefer a walking or driving tour.

- Ask your candidates how they prefer to deliver presentations—do they prefer standing, do they need a podium, or do they prefer to be sitting while presenting their work?

- Ask your candidates about any audio-visual or other equipment they may need. If they need to connect to a projection or other device, be sure to ask about which computer operating system they use (PC/Mac/other) so that you can have the necessary equipment, software, and connections available.

6. **Carefully select the location for group interviews, research presentations, and other events**

   As soon as you have dates confirmed for your candidates' visits, secure reservations for any rooms you will need. Select rooms for your events with the following considerations in mind:

   - Is the room equipped with effective temperature controls?

- Does the room have comfortable and adequate seating to accommodate the audience you expect?

- Is the room equipped with appropriate audio-visual equipment, or can the necessary equipment be provided?

- Will the room allow the candidates and all participants to adequately see and hear each other?

- Are the room and the building accessible to people with disabilities?

- What types of photographs or pictures are hanging in the room or in the hallways leading to the room? Recognize that while it is admirable to honor your predecessors by showcasing photographs of the founders of your field, past presidents or department chairs, prominent donors, and others, these photographs typically do not reflect the diversity you might be seeking. Showcasing pictures or photographs representing only or mostly majority members of the department or discipline may lead women and members of underrepresented groups to believe that they do not belong in your department or institution. This sense of not belonging can not only have a negative influence on a candidate's performance during a job interview or research talk, but may also influence a candidate's decision to accept or reject a position in your department should you make an offer.[7]

If the rooms you typically use for departmental events do not adequately meet the needs described above, investigate options for using other rooms. Aim to provide consistency between candidates visits by using the same rooms for each candidate.

7. **Provide candidates with opportunities to seek out information about your campus and community**

- **Develop an information packet to share with all candidates.** This packet can include information about your department, campus, and community. It should provide candidates with references and resources that will help them determine how well your department, campus, and community meets their personal and professional needs. For personal needs in particular, providing candidates with an information packet allows them to learn about resources, programs, and facilities without needing to discuss their personal lives with members of the search committee. For suggestions on what to include in an information packet, see "Materials to Include in an Informational Packet," p. 101.

- **Provide time in your schedule of events for your candidates to meet with someone who can provide information about campus and community resources.** Candidates may not want to ask members of the search committee questions about services and/or programs that will address their personal needs. They may worry that discussing personal needs or interests with search committee members will influence evaluation of their suitability for the job. In addition to providing an information packet, search committees can schedule a meeting for all final candidates with someone qualified to provide them with information, referrals, or resources about diverse communities, university policies, childcare, dual careers, religious services, and more. This person could be a member of

7. Sapna Cheryan, Victoria C. Plaut, Paul G. Davies, and Claude M. Steele, "Ambient Belonging: How Stereotypical Cues Impact Gender Participation in Computer Science," *Journal of Personality and Social Psychology* 97;6 (2009): 1045-1060; Claude M. Steele, "A Threat in the Air: How Stereotypes Shape Intellectual Identity and Performance," *American Psychologist* 52;6 (1997): 613-629.

the school or college's equity or diversity committee, a member of the Human Resources department, or a dean in academic affairs. It is important that this individual be uninvolved in the evaluation process and that all matters discussed be kept strictly confidential. It is also important that this opportunity be offered to all candidates—not just to those the committee assumes have need of this information—because it is impossible to know the personal needs of any one candidate. For a sample letter inviting candidates to discuss campus resources and programs, see "Sample Letter to Include in an Information Packet," p. 102. If a candidate has no specific issues to discuss relating to diversity, childcare, dual careers, or other matters, the person he or she meets with can serve as a neutral source of information about the department, college, and community. An alternative to scheduling a meeting with a particular individual is to invite the candidate to choose to meet with someone listed in the information packet, and to identify in advance a block of time the candidate can use to set up such a meeting.

8. **Prepare your candidates for the interview**
Provide candidates with a detailed schedule that identifies by name and affiliation each person who will interview them and a brief explanation of why this person is interviewing them. Providing this information to candidates in advance will allow them to prepare for their interviews by learning more about their interviewers.

9. **Prepare interviewers, colleagues, students, and others for the candidates' visits**

- **Provide interviewers with information about the candidate and the position.** To help your interviewers conduct an effective interview, provide them with copies of the job description and evaluation criteria, the candidate's curriculum vitae, any other relevant application materials, and the schedule for the candidate's visit. Provide these materials to your interviewers in advance, allowing them sufficient time for review.

  Consider supplementing the application materials with a brief biography of or introduction to the candidate and a brief description of the job. These brief documents will be helpful not only to interviewers who fail to take the time to adequately review candidates' materials, but also to others who will interact with your candidates in less formal settings. They may help your faculty, staff, and students avoid making embarrassing mistakes such as discussing the strength of your mentoring programs for junior faculty with a youthful-looking scholar who is actually interviewing for a very distinguished senior professorship, or from expecting a stronger record of publication from a mature candidate who is a recent graduate interviewing for an assistant professorship.

- **Provide guidance and suggestions for interview questions.** Encourage your interviewers to avoid asking questions readily answered in the application materials. Such questions will suggest to candidates that the interviewer has not read their materials and will not provide a good impression of the university. It is far more effective to formulate questions tailored to the research, teaching, and other interests and experiences described in each candidate's application materials.

  Consider providing your interviewers with suggested questions you would like them to address. Some interviewers will greatly appreciate your suggestions. Others will prefer to formulate their own questions, so be sure to communicate that your questions are suggestions only. Avoid providing the same set of suggested questions to every interviewer. Candidates will quickly tire of repeatedly addressing the same questions. Instead, consider asking interviewers to focus on a specific aspect of the evaluation. For example, some interviewers could concentrate on questions relating to research, or on specific aspects of research such as methodology, theoretical foundations or implications of the candidate's research, their findings or conclusions, or potential sources of funding. Others could pose questions relating primarily to teaching, or to specific aspects of teaching such as personal teaching philosophies, issues of pedagogy, curriculum development, or preferred course texts. In addition to providing a more invigorating and less tedious interview process for your candidates, this approach may provide the search committee with considerably richer and broader feedback from their interviewers.

- **Provide information about appropriate and inappropriate questions.** Provide all interviewers—and anyone else who will interact with your candidates—with a list of appropriate and inappropriate questions. Inappropriate questions include those related to age, race, ethnicity, disabilities, marital status, sexual orientation, religion, or other personal factors. See pp. 98-99 for detailed information about appropriate and inappropriate questions. Remind everyone to refrain from asking inappropriate questions not only during formal interview settings, but also during informal social events.

- **Clarify expectations for feedback.** Provide your interviewers with information about what type of feedback you expect from them and when you expect it. Will you request verbal feedback, a written evaluation, or a completed evaluation form? Whatever type of feedback you prefer, make sure that your interviewers understand you are seeking feedback regarding how well they believe each candidate meets the evaluation criteria established for the position. As discussed in Element IV, it is helpful to collect feedback as soon after each candidate's visit as possible. Establish firm deadlines for receiving feedback.

During: Guidelines for Interviewing

Guidelines: Interviews by telephone, videoconference or online video, and at academic conferences

1. **Begin the interview with introductions and welcoming statements**
   The lead interviewer, usually the search committee chair, should begin the interview by introducing him- or herself, welcoming the candidate, and introducing the other interview participants. Once these introductions are complete the lead interviewer should briefly review the plan for the interview with the candidate by confirming approximately how long the interview will take, the general topics to be discussed, and the format that will be used.

2. **Practice good etiquette**

   - **For telephone interviews:** If various members of the committee will be asking questions, each person should introduce themselves before speaking. If committee members will gather in one room around a single telephone, minimize ambient noise by avoiding the rustling of paper, tapping of fingers or pens, eating, and drinking—except perhaps for an occasional sip of a beverage. If committee members will dial in to a teleconference from their own phones, each member can minimize noise by muting their phone when not speaking. All committee members should avoid interrupting or talking over the candidate or other members of the committee.

   - **For videoconference or online video interviews:** All search committee members should be aware of and adhere to commonly accepted standards of videoconferencing etiquette and should avoid interrupting or talking over the candidate or other members of the committee. See "Video Conferencing Etiquette," p. 94.

- **For interviews at academic conferences:** Focus attention on the interview and avoid engaging in other tasks such as checking email and/or phone messages. Consider designating one person as responsible for handling essential phone calls such as those related to scheduling additional interviews and try to make such calls as unobtrusive as possible. Avoid eating and drinking during the interview.

3. **Rely on a designated timekeeper**
   Rely on non-verbal signals from a designated timekeeper to move from one topic to the next to ensure that you complete the agenda for the interview.

4. **Answer your candidate's questions to the best of your ability**
   Provide time for the candidate to ask questions and answer these to the best of your ability. If the candidate asks a question you cannot answer or cannot answer completely, let the candidate know that you will find someone to provide an answer and follow through by doing so.

5. **Conclude the interview by letting the candidate know what to expect next**
   Conclude the interview by thanking the candidate and letting him or her know about the next steps in your search process and about when to expect further communication about their candidacy.

Guidelines: On-campus interviews

1. **Hold an introductory meeting with each candidate**
   Begin the interview process by meeting with your candidate to welcome him or her and to review the plan for the day. Use this opportunity to inform the candidate about any necessary changes in the schedule previously shared, to provide any advice or insights you wish to share, and to answer any questions he or she may have. Be sure to provide all visiting candidates with the same information and advice.

2. **Follow the plan you previously established**
   In accordance with your original plan, allow enough time for interviews, follow-up questions, candidates' questions, and breaks.

3. **Make candidates feel welcome and comfortable**
   It is critical to treat all candidates fairly and with respect. If you have reason to believe that a particular interviewer may be hostile to hiring women and/or minority faculty members, don't leave the candidate alone with this interviewer. If, despite your efforts to prepare your interviewers, an interviewer asks an inappropriate question or makes racist or sexist remarks, immediately take positive and assertive steps to defuse the situation. Similarly, if a particular individual is known for taking an abrasive approach to interviewing, forewarn your candidates that this is the approach he or she takes with all candidates and advise them not to interpret the approach as a personal attack.

4. **Remind interviewers and faculty members to treat all candidates as potential colleagues**
   Whether hired by your department or not, each candidate that visits your campus is a potential colleague—either a departmental colleague or a member of your professional association. As such, repeated interactions with the candidate and his or her colleagues and students are likely. For this reason, in addition to determining the candidates' qualifications for the position you are offering, you want to provide every candidate with a good impression of your institution and its faculty. Failing to treat all candidates with respect and dignity can do lasting damage to a department and institution's reputation.

5. **Encourage all departmental faculty members to attend candidates' presentations**
   Ensuring a good turnout for all candidates' research talks can help the candidates feel welcome and respected. In addition, if departmental faculty play a role in evaluating candidates for the position, their presence is crucial.

6. **Encourage professional behavior during candidates' presentations**
   Remind all attendees of candidates' presentations to show respect for the candidates by silencing cell phones or pagers, turning off electronic devices, refraining from engaging in other tasks (e.g., reading papers, grading exams, and more), and giving their full attention to candidates' talks.

7. **Answer your candidates' questions to the best of your ability**
   Provide time for each candidate to ask questions and answer these to the best of your ability. If a candidate asks a question you cannot answer or cannot answer completely, let him or her know that you will find someone to provide an answer and follow through by doing so. If the question relates to personal items—to items that would not be appropriate for a search committee member to raise or ask—answer as fully as you can, but avoid broadening the discussion beyond the specific question the candidate asked. For example, if a candidate asked about the quality of public schools, it is not acceptable to ask if he or she has children or if a candidate asked about the availability of childcare on campus, it is not acceptable to ask about his or her partner.

8. **Avoid nudging or pressuring candidates to request assistance with dual career hiring**
   If your campus provides new hires with assistance in securing employment for their partners, include information about your program in the packet of materials you provide to candidates. Many search committees and department chairs also call attention to these resources or programs during the on-campus visit. As long as the same information is provided to all visiting candidates, it is perfectly acceptable to highlight such campus programs and to encourage all candidates to learn more about available resources. It is not acceptable, however, to urge or pressure candidates to request assistance with dual career hiring before they receive a job offer.

   Some search committee and department chairs correctly argue that the sooner they know about the need for dual career hiring assistance the more likely they are to accommodate this need successfully. They consequently believe that it is in candidates' best interests to request such assistance as soon as possible—and may urge them to do so. This approach, however, does not take into consideration concerns candidates may have about making such a request before receiving a job offer. Above all, candidates worry that this request could bias the committee's evaluation of their suitability for the position. As the research described in Element III demonstrates, when gender identity is highlighted, as it would be in a discussion of dual career hires, women are usually evaluated more negatively, especially for positions that are typically held by men. In addition, all candidates—men and women—may fear that the extra work involved in securing employment for a partner may unintentionally bias a committee's assessment of their candidacy. Concerns about the potential role of bias are legitimate reasons for waiting to receive an offer before requesting assistance with dual career hiring.

   Search committees, department chairs, and deans involved in hiring should respect candidates' concerns and their rights to avoid discussing personal needs until after receiving a job offer. Indeed, many department chairs point out that because a great deal of work and negotiation can be involved in securing employment for a candidate's partner, they are not likely to begin this process unless they are confident that their department will indeed make an offer to the candidate—in which case they might as well make the offer first.

9. **Remind interviewers to provide feedback**
    Remind interviewers and others participating in events with your candidates of the importance of providing feedback in a timely manner. Provide them with evaluation forms or other information about how to evaluate candidates and follow through by collecting feedback promptly.

10. **Conclude the interview by letting the candidate know what to expect next**
    Conclude the interview by thanking the candidate, letting him or her know approximately when to expect further communication about their candidacy, who will be making this contact, and who to contact if additional questions arise.

After: Evaluating the Interviewed Candidates

Evaluating: Interviews by telephone, videoconference or online video, and at academic conferences

1. **Review the strengths and weakness of each candidate at the conclusion of each interview**
    At the conclusion of each interview, set aside time for each member of the search committee or interview team to assess the candidate's strengths and weaknesses. Once everyone has had a chance to do this, engage in a group discussion of the assessments. Avoid making comparisons between candidates until all interviews are complete.

2. **After all interviews are complete, meet to discuss and compare candidates**

    - **Review Element IV: Ensure a Fair and Thorough Review of Applicants.** Pay particular attention to the advice for Stage 3 of the evaluation process, pp. 56-58.

    - **Follow the agreed-upon process for making decisions about selecting final candidates.** Evaluate candidates for their strengths and weaknesses on specific job-related attributes and be able to defend every decision for including or excluding a candidate.

3. **Communicate with your candidates in a timely manner**
    Contact your candidates within the time frame you initially established. If you have not made your decision within this time frame, let them know that the process is ongoing and provide them with a revised timeline for a decision. If you have made some decisions, communicate promptly with candidates you are considering further and send appropriate notification to candidates you are no longer considering (see Element IV, "Sample Letters to Applicants," pp. 69-71).

Evaluating: On-campus interviews

1. **Meet with your search committee as soon as possible after the completion of each visit**
    Meet to evaluate each candidate at the conclusion of his or her visit. Doing so promptly can maximize recall and minimize bias. Similarly, any feedback sought from other groups or individuals with whom the candidate met should be collected and assessed as soon after the candidate's visit as possible. Strive to focus on the strengths and weaknesses of each individual candidate and avoid making comparisons between candidates until all interviews are complete.

2. **Follow your committee's agreed-upon process for making hiring decisions**
   Evaluate candidates for their strengths and weaknesses on specific job-related attributes. Be able to justify every decision on the basis of evidence drawn from the candidates' applications materials and from their performance during interviews.

3. **Review the materials for Element III: Raise awareness of unconscious assumptions and their influence on evaluation of applicants**
   Carefully question your judgments and consider whether any assumptions or biases are influencing your evaluation of final candidates.

4. **Establish a procedure for checking references**
   Consistent with the advice to treat all candidates equitably, if your committee conducts reference checks, it should establish a common process for all candidates. The committee should discuss what information it hopes to obtain, develop a set of questions designed to provide this information, determine which references to contact, and designate members to conduct the inquiry. As you develop questions for reference checking, remember that questions that are inappropriate to ask of candidates are also inappropriate to ask of their references. If someone should share with you personal information about a candidate (such as their age, marital status, sexual orientation, religious affiliation or other categories protected by federal and state equal opportunity laws) even though you did not ask for it, avoid relying on this information in your evaluation.

   If you plan to conduct interviews with individuals other than references your candidates identified, let your candidates know. Consider providing them with an opportunity to consent to your proposed list of references, or to explain why they might prefer you not to contact any particular individual. It is entirely possible that references you have identified may not provide fair recommendations—they may have biases of their own that can influence their assessments of your candidates.

5. **Communicate with both successful and unsuccessful candidates in a timely manner**
   Contact your candidates within the time frame you initially established to offer them a position, or to let them know that another candidate has received and accepted an offer. If you have not made your decision yet, let your candidates know that you are still considering them for the position and provide a revised timeline for a decision. If you have already selected a candidate and made an offer, but have not received an acceptance from the selected candidate, refer to advice on "Maintaining communication" in Element VI: Close the Deal: Successfully Hire Your Selected Candidate, p. 107. (See also: Element IV, "Sample Letters to Applicants," pp. 69-71.)

6. **Decide how to proceed if your top candidate turns you down**
   As a committee, discuss the possibility that your selected candidate may not accept your job offer. Consult with your department chair and/or the dean of your school or college, to determine how you will proceed in such a situation. Will the department make an offer to another candidate, re-open the search, or make a temporary hire? If there is any possibility that the department will make an offer to one of your other final candidates, it is particularly important to heed the advice provided in Element VI, p. 107, about communicating with your final candidates.

RESOURCES

Advice for Interviewing

Prepare for the interview

From the UW–Madison Office of Quality Improvement and Office of Human Resource Development
http://go.wisc.edu/b40923

All members of the interview team at this stage should clearly understand the criteria that will be used to evaluate the applicants.

1. Read the résumés ahead of time and write your thoughts on them. Use question marks where you want more info.

2. Formulate questions and write them down before the interview.

3. Ask the same questions of each applicant applying for the job. (Variations would occur with the specific backgrounds of each applicant and variations in a person's method of answering the questions.)

4. It is important to be a good listener, not only to learn the most you can about the person, but undivided attention of the interviewers will make the applicant feel more at ease and open up.

5. Don't look impatient or bored. Don't play with paper clips, rubber bands, pencils, etc. The applicant will tense up and not respond with information you might be looking for.

6. Do not take extensive notes. This will make the applicant tense up and stop talking. If you think of a question, just jot down a quick word or two to remind you of what popped into your head and then continue to listen. Record your thoughts and evaluate the applicant right after the interview.

7. Phrase questions in such a way that will lead the applicant to do most of the talking. Keep questions short and direct. If the applicant gets off the point of the question (gently) lead them back on to it.

8. Don't ask questions that can be answered with a simple "yes" or "no"; and don't ask leading questions that telegraph the answer you want, e.g., "We have a team approach here ... how do you feel about that?"

Compiled by Bruce Hellmich, Assistant Dean, School of Human Ecology, UW–Madison, 2002.

RESOURCES

Video Conferencing Etiquette

By Kathy McCain

Reprinted with permission from the UW-Madison Department of Family Medicine
https://inside.fammed.wisc.edu/documents/3447

The most important thing to remember is:

Someone is looking at you!!

Dos and Don'ts:

- DO speak naturally and clearly
- DO engage others
- DO mute your microphone when not in use
- DO silence cell phones, watch alarms, pagers
- DO identify yourself
- DO wait for person to finish talking
- DO maintain eye contact with camera

- DO NOT tap fingers, pens
- DO NOT rustle papers
- DO NOT cover the microphone
- DO NOT make broad, wild gestures
- DO NOT engage in side conversations

Additional Don'ts:

- DO NOT check e-mail or visit websites
- DO NOT eat food or snacks

RESOURCES

Sample Interview Questions

Before developing your interview questions, review the description you created for the position and the list of evaluation criteria you developed. Rely on these documents to craft your interview questions. Your questions should elicit answers that will enable you to evaluate candidates on the basis of the criteria you have developed. Interview questions generally fall into three major categories: research, teaching, and academic service. Some sample questions and links to many more available on the web are provided below. This list is not intended to be comprehensive, but rather to provide suggestions you can adapt and add to as you develop questions relevant to your search.

Research & Publications:

(For junior scholars):
Tell us about your dissertation: What led you to choose this topic? What research methodology did you use and why? What contributions does your dissertation (and/or other publications) make to the field?

(For senior scholars):
What do you consider to be your major contributions to the field? What led you to choose this topic/these topics? What research methodologies do you use and why? How has your work contributed to the field?

(For all candidates):
What directions do you see your research taking in the next 5-10 years? What is the topic of your next major research proposal and how do you anticipate funding it?

What publications or other academic products do you have in the pipeline (e.g., books, articles, online or web-based publications, patents, creative and artistic works, outreach materials, curricula or other educational materials)?

Describe your experience with interdisciplinary research and/or teaching activities. If none, what interests do you have in interdisciplinary collaboration and how would you establish interdisciplinary connections?

Teaching:

How has your experience and training prepared you to teach the courses required? What books or other materials would you select for Course X, and why?

What other courses would you like to teach or develop?

Tell us how your research has influenced your teaching. In what ways have you been able to bring the insights of your research to your courses at the graduate level? At the undergraduate level?

What is your teaching philosophy? How does it influence your teaching and curriculum development?

RESOURCES

Please describe efforts you have made to adapt your teaching for students with a variety of different learning styles.

Please give some examples indicating your ability to work effectively with students from diverse backgrounds.

What strategies have you used to develop inclusive learning environments?

What experiences have you had mentoring or advising students? Please describe some challenges you have encountered. Please describe some successes of which you are proud.

Community/Service:

Please describe some strategies you have used to enhance the professional advancement or academic success of individuals from groups that are underrepresented in your institution?

What experiences or interests do you have in campus-wide activities and service?

What experience or interests do you have in outreach or service activities, beyond your campus?

In what ways do you cultivate and maintain professional networks? How does this contribute to or support your teaching, research, or service?

How would you like to see yourself continue to develop as a faculty member at this institution?

General:

Why do you want to join our faculty?

Why are you interested in this position, and what about the position attracts you most?

How do you see yourself contributing to this position? To the department? To the institution as a whole?

(After describing the broader mission of the institution) How would your research and or teaching foster the mission of the institution?

Useful Websites:

Note: Many of these websites aim to provide advice to job applicants, but the information they provide about interview questions can also be of use to search committees.

- Mary Corbin Sies, Dept. of American Studies, University of Maryland, College Park, "Questions one should be prepared to answer for job interviews":
  http://otal.umd.edu/~sies/jobquess.html

- Kathryn L. Cottingham, Biological Sciences, Dartmouth College. "Questions to ask (and be prepared to answer) during an academic interview":
  http://graduate.dartmouth.edu/careers/services/interview/acad.html#preparation

RESOURCES

- On the Cutting Edge: Professional Development for Geoscience Faculty, "Some Typical Academic Interview Questions": http://serc.carleton.edu/NAGTWorkshops/careerprep/jobsearch/interviewquestions.html

- The Chronicle Forums: "List of Phone Interview Questions": http://chronicle.com/forums/index.php/topic,64844.0.html

RESOURCES

Appropriate and Inappropriate Interview Questions

Reproduced, with minor adaptations, from the University of Wisconsin–Madison Office of Human Resources (http://go.wisc.edu/54sqgx)

Rules to Remember

1. Ask only what you need to know, not what you would like to know.
   - Need to know: affects the day-to-day requirements of the job.
   - Like to know: does not pertain to the job, usually personal in nature.
2. If you have any questions about the appropriateness of the question, don't ask it.
3. If you ask a question to one candidate, you must ask the question to ALL candidates.

SUBJECT	INAPPROPRIATE	APPROPRIATE
AGE	Questions about age, dates of attending school, dates of military service, request for birth certificate.	Questions about age are only permitted to ensure that a person is legally old enough to do the job.
ADDRESS	Examples: Do you own or rent your home? How long have you lived at your current address?	What is your address?
ARREST RECORD and CONVICTIONS	Questions about arrests, pending charges and convictions that do not relate substantially to the job. Example: Have you ever been arrested?	Varies by state. Some states permit questions that relate substantially to the particular job if they are asked of all candidates. Check with the Legal Affairs or Equal Opportunity Office of your institution.
CREDIT RATINGS or GARNISHMENTS	Questions that have no relation to job performance. Refusing to hire someone based on a poor credit rating is a civil rights violation.	Questions may be appropriate if the job requires significant financial responsibility. In most cases, no question is acceptable.
CITIZENSHIP	Any question about citizenship. Examples: Are you a US citizen? Where were you born? Are you an American? What kind of name is that?	May ask about legal authorization to work in a specific position, if all applicants are asked.
DISABILITY	Questions about disability are not appropriate. Examples: Do you have a disability? What is the nature or severity of your disability? Do you have a health condition? Do you require accommodations?	Questions about ability are appropriate. Example: Are you able to perform the essential functions of this job, with or without accommodations?

RESOURCES

SUBJECT	INAPPROPRIATE	APPROPRIATE
EDUCATION	Questions about education that are not related to the job being applied for.	Inquiries about degrees or equivalent experience related to the job being applied for.
FAMILY or MARITAL STATUS	Any inquiry about marital status, pregnancy, children, or child care plans.	Questions about whether an applicant can meet work schedules or job requirements if asked of all candidates, both men and women.
HEALTH	Any question about health. Examples: How is your health? How is your family's health?	None.
MILITARY SERVICE	Any question about type of discharge or registration status. Example: Were you honorably discharged from military service?	Questions about education and experience acquired in the military that relate to a particular job.
NAME	Questions about national origin, ancestry, or prior marital status. Examples: What kind of a name is that? Is that your maiden name?	May ask about current legal name. Example: Is additional information, such as a different name or nickname necessary in order to check job references?
NATIONAL ORIGIN	Any questions about national origin or citizenship. Examples: Are you legally eligible to work in the U.S.A.? Where were you or your parents born? What is your native language?	May ask if legally authorized to work in this specific position, if all applicants are asked this question.
ORGANIZATIONS	Inquiries about membership in organizations that might indicate race, sex, religion, or national origin.	Inquiries about membership in professional organizations related to the position.
RACE, COLOR, HEIGHT, WEIGHT	Questions about complexion, color, height, or weight.	None.
SEXUAL ORIENTATION	Any question about sexual orientation. Examples: Are you gay? Why do you wear an earring?	None.
WORK EXPERIENCE	Inquiries posed to members of minority groups based on generalizations or stereotypes of the group. Examples: Questions about use of sick leave, or worker's compensation	Questions about applicants' previous employment experience.

RESOURCES

Tips for Interviewing Applicants with Disabilities

Reproduced, with minor adaptations, from the University of Wisconsin–Madison Office of Human Resources' Recruitment Toolkit**
http://go.wisc.edu/5fv984

In addition to being uncertain about what questions may and may not be asked when interviewing an applicant with a disability, interviewers are often unsure of "disability etiquette" when interacting with people who have disabilities. These guidelines are provided to improve communication and interactions.

When interviewing an applicant with any disability

- Don't ask: "What happened to you?" or: "Do you have a disability?" or: "How will you get to work?"
- Don't ask questions phrased in terms of disability: "Do you have a medical condition that would preclude you from qualifying for this position?"
- Do ask job-related questions: "How would you perform this particular task?"
- Don't ask: "How often will you require leave for treatment of your condition?" However, you may state the organization's attendance requirements and ask if the applicant can meet them.
- Don't try to elicit the applicant's needs for accommodation. The interview should focus on whether the candidate is otherwise qualified for the job in question. Focus on the applicant's need for accommodation ONLY if there is an obvious disability, or if the applicant discloses a disability or need for accommodation.
- Always offer to shake hands. Do not avoid eye contact, but don't stare either.
- Treat the applicant as you would any other adult—don't be patronizing. If you don't usually address applicants by their first name, don't make an exception for applicants with disabilities.
- If you feel it appropriate, offer the applicant assistance (for example, if an individual with poor grasping ability has trouble opening a door), but don't assume it will necessarily be accepted. Don't automatically give assistance without asking first.
- Whenever possible, let the applicant visit the actual workplace.

When interviewing an applicant who uses a wheelchair

- Don't lean on the wheelchair.
- Don't be embarrassed to use such phrases as "Let's walk over to the plant."
- Be sure to speak and interact at eye level with the applicant if the conversation lasts more than a couple of minutes.

**Excerpted from: MIN Report #7—July–August 1991, Governor's Committee for People With Disabilities. 1 W. Wilson Street, Room 558, P.O. Box 7852, Madison, WI. 53707.

RESOURCES

Materials to Include in an Informational Packet

- Information about your university, its governance and structure.

- Information about your department, its governance and structure.

- Information about employee benefits and leave policies.

- A letter from your school or college's Equity and Diversity Committee (or some other relevant individual or organization not directly involved in the search) indicating that the candidate may have a confidential discussion or meeting with them to learn about campus and community resources and programs. (See "Sample Letter to Include in an Informational Packet," p. 102.)

- Information from or about campus offices and organizations responsible for equity, diversity, and inclusion.

- Information from or about campus offices or programs providing services or resources for people with disabilities.

- Information from or about campus organizations for members of LGBTQ (Lesbian, Gay, Bisexual, Transgender, Queer) communities.

- Information from or about campus offices or resources for childcare and work-life balance.

- Information about campus programs for dual career couples.

- Information about faculty development, mentoring and support programs—especially programs for women faculty and faculty who belong to minority groups if these are available on your campus.

- Information about your community including:

  o Cultural and community organizations, events, and resources
  o Neighborhoods
  o Public and private schools
  o Religious organizations and institutions
  o Resources for childcare and eldercare
  o Resources for people with disabilities
  o Resources for members of LGBTQ communities
  o Local attractions and restaurants
  o Ethnic grocery stores, beauticians, and barbers
  o Media outlets serving diverse communities (e.g., a Hispanic radio station, a newspaper covering issues and events of particular relevance to the local African American community, or a magazine focusing on LGBTQ issues and events)

RESOURCES

Sample Letter to Include in an Informational Packet

Adapted from a letter written by Mariamne Whatley for the University of Wisconsin–Madison School of Education's Equity and Diversity Committee.

Dear (Name of candidate)

The members of (Name of committee) wish to assist you in your efforts to become more acquainted with the (Name of university or college) and with (Name of city or town). We hope you find this packet of information (or our informational webpage) helpful.

Please let us know if there is any further information we can provide. You should feel free to ask for specific information that you may need about the (Name of school or college), (Name of university), or (Name of city or town).

In addition, we can provide personal answers to questions that you or anyone moving with you may have about such matters as child care, housing, elder care, or employment opportunities. If you would like to talk with a member of the (Name of committee), please contact (Name and phone number or email of contact person). He or she can arrange for you to talk with a committee member with whom you can have a complete, confidential, and informal discussion of your concerns.

Sincerely,

(Name)
(Title)

Enclosures: Information Packet

VI. CLOSE THE DEAL: SUCESSFULLY HIRE YOUR SELECTED CANDIDATE

Make your offer promptly (p. 104)

Give candidates sufficient time to consider the offer (p. 104)

Offer prospective faculty members a second campus visit (p. 105)

Dual career hiring: Opportunities and challenges (p. 105)

Negotiating the offer (pp. 106–107)

Maintaining communication (p. 107)

Welcoming the new faculty member (p. 108)

Some search committees consider their work complete once the committee or the department reaches a final decision and makes an offer to one or more candidates. At this point, the department chair usually takes the primary role in communicating and negotiating with selected candidates. Search committees, however, can play an influential role in helping selected candidates decide to accept a position. Indeed, because search committee members have invested considerable time and effort throughout the process, they have an interest in reaching a successful conclusion and hiring the candidates they worked to select. Several factors that can contribute to successfully hiring selected candidates are discussed below.

Make your offer promptly

Once all interviews with your final candidates are complete, conduct your evaluations and make your decisions as promptly as possible. As recommended in Element I, understand the role your committee will play in determining who receives an offer and know what steps and approvals are required to make an official offer. Be prepared to provide a thorough, well-documented, and convincing case for your committee's decisions and choices. Though the search committee will not necessarily have control over the timing of the approval process, knowing what that process is, who the responsible parties are, and how much time it should take will allow the search committee to monitor the process and help ensure that it proceeds smoothly. This knowledge will also enable the search committee to provide candidates with reasonable estimates of when to expect a response.

Providing selected candidates with an offer as soon after their visit as possible is one way of increasing the chances that they will accept a position. Timely offers convey to candidates the clear message of your eagerness to have them join your department. Conversely, candidates who do not receive a timely response, especially if they do not receive a response within the timeframe you initially provided, will start to assume you are no longer interested in their candidacy.

Give candidates sufficient time to consider the offer

Work with your department chair, dean, or other relevant administrative leader to establish a reasonable timeframe for candidates to respond to the offer. Clearly, it is in the department and institution's best interest to receive an answer as soon as possible. If the selected candidate accepts the position, the search can conclude by sending rejection notices to other candidates. If the selected candidate rejects the position, the committee or department may still have time to make an offer to a different candidate.

Nevertheless, it is important for committees, departments, and administrators to understand that prospective faculty members need adequate time to make a decision. Many factors may be involved in their decisions. They may be waiting on offers from other institutions, they may need to investigate employment opportunities for a spouse or partner, and they may need to consider how well your institution and community meets their family and personal needs.

Balancing the competing needs of the institution and the candidates is essential for establishing a reasonable deadline for a response. Pressuring a candidate who is not yet ready to decide will not benefit anyone. The candidate may decide to wait for an offer from an institution that is more considerate of his or her needs, or may accept the offer only to subsequently discover that the institution or community is not a good fit and begin seeking a new position causing the department to start the search all over again.

Offer prospective faculty members a second campus visit

Many departments invite prospective faculty members for a second campus visit to help them make a decision about accepting an offer. If the prospective faculty member has a spouse or partner, he or she frequently also participates in this visit. A second visit offers prospective candidates excellent opportunities to learn more about their potential colleagues, the department, the university, and the community. Search committee members can play a pivotal role in making a prospective faculty member and his or her partner or spouse feel welcome and can provide valuable information about the campus and community. These conversations and the sharing of information, perspectives, and resources can be more open and forthright than during the evaluation process and can help prospective faculty members learn about how or if the campus and community will meet their personal, family, and professional needs.

Understandably, budgetary constraints will determine a department's ability to arrange a second visit for a prospective candidate. However, the costs of a second visit represent a rather small investment in a new faculty member who will likely contribute many years to the department, and are considerably less expensive than hiring a faculty member who leaves after a year or two because the college or community does not fit his or her professional or personal goals or needs.

Dual career hiring: Opportunities and challenges

Recognizing that prospective faculty members often have an equally talented and qualified spouse or partner who is also seeking employment, many campuses offer programs and resources designed to help find employment for the spouse or partner. The existence of these programs and the support they provide can be very attractive to prospective faculty members and can often influence their decisions to accept an offer—especially if the efforts to find employment for a spouse or partner are successful. Indeed, a recent study concluded that universities risk "losing prized candidates if suitable employment cannot be found for a partner."[1]

However, efforts to find employment for a spouse or partner can take time and can lead prospective faculty members to postpone making a decision to accept an offer. The process of pursuing employment opportunities for a spouse or partner, consequently, can interfere with a search committee or departments' goal of timeliness. Universities with clear and established policies and procedures in place for dual-career hiring can minimize the time it takes to determine if they can offer a position to a spouse or partner, but all committees and departments must consider how to respond to other candidates during the interim.[2] (See "Maintaining Communication," p. 107.)

---

1. Londa Schiebinger, Andrea Davies Henderson, and Shannon K. Gilmartin, *Dual-Career Academic Couples: What Universities Need to Know* (Stanford, CA: Michelle R. Clayman Institute for Gender Research, Stanford University, 2008), 6.

2. Suggestions and guidelines for establishing effective dual-career hiring programs are provided in Schiebinger, Henderson, and Gilmartin, *Dual-Career Academic Couples.*

Negotiating the offer

Negotiations between department chairs and prospective faculty members about salary, start-up funding, and other issues also influence candidates' decisions about accepting an offer and can delay the successful conclusion of a search. While department chairs must obviously consider the limits of their departments' resources, these negotiations are more likely to lead to successfully hiring and retaining desirable faculty members if they keep not only the bottom line, but also the success of new faculty members in mind. As they negotiate, department chairs should ensure that new faculty members receive the resources they need to be successful and that resources are equitably distributed among new hires in the department.

Search committee members are typically not involved in this negotiation process, but they can reiterate for the chair the reasons they chose and are eager to hire a particular candidate. They and the department chair should also be aware that women and members of minority groups may have received less mentoring and preparation for negotiating an offer than have men from majority groups. To ensure equity in the negotiation process, scholars at the University of Michigan suggest providing all prospective faculty members with a list of items commonly discussed during negotiations. This could include salary, start-up funds, course release time, laboratory space and equipment, clerical or administrative support, and more.[3]

In addition, department chairs and search committee members should be aware that the same powerful social and cultural norms that lead to unconscious bias in evaluations influence both women's inclinations to negotiate on their own behalf and responses to women's efforts to negotiate for their own benefit. A study of starting salaries and negotiating practices of students who graduated with master's degrees from Carnegie Mellon University, for example, found that on average men's salaries were 7.6% (approximately $4,000) higher than women's salaries and that 57% of the male graduates had negotiated for higher salaries compared to only 7% of the female graduates. Subsequent studies confirmed women's reluctance to negotiate salaries.[4]

Women are quite successful at negotiating on behalf of others, which aligns well with social assumptions and expectations that women are and should be kind, nice, sympathetic, selfless, and supportive of others. Negotiating on one's own behalf, however, requires one to be more assertive, aggressive, competitive, and self-oriented—traits more commonly associated with and expected of men. As noted in Element III, though individual women and men differ in the extent to which they adhere to these gender norms, these widely held assumptions influence reactions to men and women who violate gender norms. Consequently, simply teaching or encouraging women to negotiate more aggressively on their own behalf is not necessarily an effective solution because women who do negotiate in this manner often encounter social and professional penalties—they are frequently considered to be demanding and domineering.[5] Indeed, a recent research study demonstrated this "penalty" by asking participants to evaluate transcripts of interviews with internal candidates who were offered a promotion. The participants, college-educated, employed adults many of whom had management experience, evaluat-

---

3. University of Michigan ADVANCE, *Handbook for Faculty Searches and Hiring, Academic Year 2009-10* (Ann Arbor: University of Michigan ADVANCE, 2009), 18, www.advance.rackham.umich.edu /handbook.pdf, accessed 5/17/2012.

4. Linda Babcock and Sara Laschever, *Women Don't Ask: Negotiation and the Gender Divide* (Princeton, NJ: Princeton University Press, 2003), 1-4.

5. For a full discussion of gender and its influence on negotiation, see Babcock and Laschever, *Women Don't Ask.*

ed candidates on a number of personality traits and on several measures designed to assess their willingness to work with the candidates. The transcripts differed only with respect to whether the name of the candidate was male or female and whether or not the candidate attempted to negotiate salary. Analysis of results showed that evaluators' willingness to work with a male candidate was not influenced by whether he did or did not attempt to negotiate salary. Evaluators, however, were substantially less willing to work with a woman who engaged in such a negotiation and rated her as more demanding and less nice than women who did not negotiate. Women's reluctance to negotiate, the authors conclude, results from the negative reactions they receive when they do.[6]

This research suggests that department chairs seeking to attract and retain excellent women faculty members will be more successful by ensuring that offers made and resources provided to women are equivalent to those made to men rather than by expecting women to negotiate aggressively on their own behalf.

Maintaining communication

If for any reason the committee or department cannot respond to final candidates in a timely manner, maintaining communication with them is critical.

If procedural complications or delays prevent the committee or department from making an offer within the timeframe initially shared with candidates, contact them—preferably by phone—to let them know that the search process is still ongoing and that you are still interested in their candidacy. Provide a revised estimate of when they should expect to hear from you again.

If the committee or department has already made an offer but is waiting for an acceptance from the selected candidate, communication with other candidates will depend upon whether or not the committee or department plans to offer the position to another candidate if the selected candidate refuses the position. If the choice is not to make an alternative offer and to run a new search the following year, promptly inform the other candidates that you have made an offer and thank them for their interest in the position.

If the committee or department is interested in making a new offer to another candidate, communication is more complicated. The committee or department will need to decide whether they want to delay any public announcements of an offer and reassure remaining candidates that the search has not yet concluded, or whether to adopt a more forthright approach and inform candidates that another candidate has received an offer but has not yet accepted the position. In the latter case, the committee or department chair can assure the remaining candidates that they will still be considered for the position should the selected candidate refuse the offer. If your discipline is sufficiently small and close-knit or has a vigorous "job rumor mill," word of your selection may become public despite the absence of any official communication or announcement. In this case, it is probably best to choose the more forthright approach. Either choice, delaying the decision or informing your candidates that an offer has been made, is better than not communicating at all and leaving candidates to assume not only that you are no longer considering them, but also that you neglected to inform them of your decision.

---

6. Hannah Riley Bowles, Linda Babcock, and Lei Lai, "Social Incentives for Gender Differences in the Propensity to Initiate Negotiations: Sometimes It Does Hurt to Ask," *Organizational Behavior and Human Decision Processes* 103;1 (2007): 84-103.

Welcoming the new faculty member

Once a new faculty member is hired, members of the search committee can help welcome the new hire to the department. They can introduce him or her to other colleagues and check-in every so often to see how the transition to the new job, new school, and new community is going. These friendly overtures can help new faculty members integrate into the department more quickly.

CONCLUSION

Hiring new faculty members provides colleges and universities with an opportunity to shape their future. New faculty are usually hired with the expectation that they will attain tenure and remain with the institution for many mutually rewarding years. They will profoundly influence the institution's reputation in both research and teaching domains. They will educate and inspire generations of students. As we become an increasingly diverse and global society, it is critically important that the faculty we hire offer excellence in research and teaching; provide a rich variety of disciplinary interests, perspectives, and personal backgrounds; reflect the diversity present in our population; and contribute to a dynamic and engaged intellectual community.

Yet, hiring new faculty is a time-consuming and expensive endeavor. A failed search represents a major loss not only of the time and money invested but also of a lost opportunity to hire a potentially valuable colleague. The costs of hiring a person who does not work out or who leaves the institution shortly after being hired can be immense. A 2010 study of faculty hiring at one large research-intensive institution reported that over 50% of offers (135 offers) included at least $100,000 in start-up costs.[1] Clearly, campuses can benefit from increasing the effectiveness and efficiency of their search processes.

It is our hope that this guidebook will provide faculty search committees with information, advice, and resources that will help them run productive and efficient searches, create diverse and excellent applicant pools, conduct fair and effective evaluations, and ultimately hire new faculty who will make substantial contributions to the excellence and diversity of their institutions.

---

1. University of Wisconsin-Madison, Office of Academic Planning and Analysis, "Summary of Faculty Recruitment Efforts," 2010-11.

BIBLIOGRAPHY

American Historical Association. "AHA Guidelines for the Hiring Process." November 26, 2011. www.historians.org/Perspectives/eib/hiring_guidelines.htm. Accessed 2/15/2012.

Babcock, Linda and Sara Laschever. *Women Don't Ask: Negotiation and the Gender Divide.* Princeton, NJ: Princeton University Press, 2003.

Banaji, Mahzarin R., Max H. Bazerman, and Dolly Chugh. "How (Un)Ethical Are You?" *Harvard Business Review* 81;12 (2003): 56-64.

Bensimon, Estela Mara, Kelly Ward, and Karla Sanders. *The Department Chair's Role in Developing New Faculty into Teachers and Scholars.* Bolton, MA: Ankar Publishing Co., 2000.

Bertrand, Marianne and Sendhil Mullainathan. "Are Emily and Greg More Employable than Lakisha and Jamal? A Field Experiment on Labor Market Discrimination." *American Economic Review* 94;4 (2004): 991-1013.

Bielby, William T. and James N. Baron. "Men and Women at Work: Sex Segregation and Statistical Discrimination." *American Journal of Sociology* 91;4 (1986): 759-799.

Biernat, Monica and Kathleen Fuegen. "Shifting Standards and the Evaluation of Competence: Complexity in Gender-Based Judgment and Decision Making." *Journal of Social Issues* 57;4 (2001): 707-724.

Biernat, Monica and Melvin Manis. "Shifting Standards and Stereotype-Based Judgments." *Journal of Personality and Social Psychology* 66;1 (1994): 5-20.

Biernat, Monica, Melvin Manis, and Thomas E. Nelson. "Stereotypes and Standards of Judgment." *Journal of Personality and Social Psychology* 60;4 (1991): 485-499.

Blair, Irene V., Jennifer E. Ma, and Alison P. Lenton. "Imagining Stereotypes Away: The Moderation of Implicit Stereotypes through Mental Imagery." *Journal of Personality and Social Psychology* 81;5 (2001): 828-841.

Bowles, Hannah Riley, Linda Babcock, and Lei Lai. "Social Incentives for Gender Differences in the Propensity to Initiate Negotiations: Sometimes It Does Hurt to Ask." *Organizational Behavior and Human Decision Processes* 103;1 (2007): 84-103.

Bragger, Jennifer DeNicolis, Eugene Kutcher, John Morgan, and Patricia Firth. "The Effects of the Structured Interview on Reducing Biases Against Pregnant Job Applicants." *Sex Roles* 46;7/8 (2002): 215-226.

Brauer, Markus and Abdelatif Er-rafiy. "Increasing Perceived Variability Reduces Prejudice and Discrimination." *Journal of Experimental Social Psychology* 47;5 (2011): 871-881.

Brown, Virginia and Florence L. Geis. "Turning Lead into Gold: Evaluations of Men and Women Leaders and the Alchemy of Social Consensus." *Journal of Personality and Social Psychology* 46;4 (1984): 811–824.

Budden, Amber E., et al. "Double-Blind Review Favours Increased Representation of Female Authors." *TRENDS in Ecology and Evolution* 23;1 (2008): 4-6.

Chang, Mitchell J., Daria Witt, James Jones, and Kenji Hakuta, eds. *Compelling Interest: Examining the Evidence on Racial Dynamics in Colleges and Universities.* Stanford, CA: Stanford University Press, 2003.

Cheryan, Sapna, Victoria C. Plaut, Paul G. Davies, and Claude M. Steele. "Ambient Belonging: How Stereotypical Cues Impact Gender Participation in Computer Science." *Journal of Personality and Social Psychology* 97;6 (2009): 1045-1060.

"Chronicle Forums: Interviewing in Hotel Room?" *Chronicle of Higher Education*. November 2007. http://chronicle.com/forums/index.php/topic,43921.0.html. Accessed 2/15/2012.

Congressional Commission on the Advancement of Women and Minorities in Science, Engineering and Technology Development (CAWMSET). *Land of Plenty: Diversity as America's Competitive Edge in Science, Engineering and Technology*. Arlington, VA: National Science Foundation, 2000. www.nsf.gov/pubs/2000/cawmset0409/cawmset_0409.pdf. Accessed 6/29/2012.

Correll, Shelley J., Stephen Benard, and In Paik. "Getting a Job: Is there a Motherhood Penalty?" *American Journal of Sociology* 112;5 (2007): 1297-1338.

Darlington, David. "AHA Today: The Job Center: What Candidates Need to Know." *American Historical Association Annual Meeting*. November 23, 2010. http://blog.historians.org/annual-meeting/1184/the-job-center-what-candidates-need-to-know. Accessed 2/15/2012.

Dasgupta, Nilanjana and Anthony G. Greenwald. "On the Malleability of Automatic Attitudes: Combating Automatic Prejudice with Images of Admired and Disliked Individuals." *Journal of Personality and Social Psychology* 81;5 (2001): 800-814.

Dobbs, Michael and William D. Crano. "Outgroup Accountability in the Minimal Group Paradigm: Implications for Aversive Discrimination and Social Identity Theory." *Personality and Social Psychology Bulletin* 27;3 (2001): 355-364.

Dovidio, John F. "On the Nature of Contemporary Prejudice: The Third Wave." *Journal of Social Issues* 57;4 (2001): 829-849.

Dovidio, John F. and Samuel L. Gaertner. "Aversive Racism and Selection Decisions: 1989 and 1999." *Psychological Science* 11;4 (2000): 315-319.

Eagly, Alice H. and Linda L. Carli. *Through the Labyrinth: The Truth About How Women Become Leaders*. Boston, MA: Harvard Business School Press, 2007.

Eagly, Alice H. and Steven J. Karau. "Role Congruity Theory of Prejudice Toward Female Leaders." *Psychological Review* 109;3 (2002): 573-598.

Fine, Eve and Jo Handelsman. *Reviewing Applicants: Research on Bias and Assumptions*. Madison, WI: Board of Regents of the University of Wisconsin System, 2012. http://wiseli.engr.wisc.edu/docs/BiasBrochure_3rdEd.pdf.

Foschi, Martha. "Double Standards in the Evaluation of Men and Women." *Social Psychology Quarterly* 59;3 (1996): 237-254.

Gailliot, Matthew T., et al. "Self-Control Relies on Glucose as a Limited Energy Source: Willpower is More than a Metaphor." *Journal of Personality and Social Psychology* 92;2 (2007): 325-336.

Gaucher, Danielle, Justin Friesen, and Aaron C. Kay. "Evidence that Gendered Wording in Job Advertisements Exists and Sustains Gender Inequality." *Journal of Personality and Social Psychology* 101;1 (2011):109-128.

Goldin, Claudia and Cecilia Rouse. "Orchestrating Impartiality: The Impact of 'Blind' Auditions on Female Musicians." *American Economic Review* 90;4 (2000): 715-741.

Heilman, Madeline E. "Description and Prescription: How Gender Stereotypes Prevent Women's Ascent Up the Organizational Ladder." *Journal of Social Issues* 57;4 (2001): 657-674.

Heilman, Madeline E. "The Impact of Situational Factors on Personnel Decisions Concerning Women: Varying the Sex Composition of the Applicant Pool." *Organizational Behavior and Human Performance* 26;3 (1980): 386-395.

Heilman, Madeline E. "Information as a Deterrent Against Sex Discrimination: The Effects of Applicant Sex and Information Type on Preliminary Employment Decisions." *Organizational Behavior and Human Performance* 33;2 (1984): 174-186.

Heilman, Madeline E., William S. Battle, Chris E. Keller, and R. Andrew Lee. "Type of Affirmative Action Policy: A Determinant of Reactions to Sex-Based Preferential Selection?" *Journal of Applied Psychology* 83;2 (1998): 190–205.

Heilman, Madeline E. and Michelle C. Haynes. "Subjectivity in the Appraisal Process: A Facilitator of Gender Bias in Work Settings." In *Beyond Common Sense: Psychological Science in the Courtroom*, edited by E. Borgida and S. T. Fiske, 127-155. Malden, MA: Blackwell Publishing, 2008.

Heilman, Madeline E., Michael C. Simon, and David P. Repper. "Intentionally Favored, Unintentionally Harmed? Impact of Sex-Based Preferential Selection on Self-Perceptions and Self-Evaluations." *Journal of Applied Psychology* 72;1 (1987): 62–68.

Heilman, Madeline E., Aaron S. Wallen, Daniella Fuchs, and Melinda M. Tamkins. "Penalties for Success: Reactions to Women Who Succeed at Male Gender-Typed Tasks." *Journal of Applied Psychology* 89;3 (2004): 416-427.

Hellmich, Bruce. "Prepare for the Interview." Madison, WI: Office of Quality Improvement and Office of Human Resource Development. http://go.wisc.edu/b4092. Accessed 9/11/2012.

Hernandez, Brigida and Katherine McDonald, eds. *Exploring the Bottom Line: A Study of the Costs and Benefits of Workers with Disabilities.* Chicago, IL: DePaul University and the Illinois Department of Commerce and Economic Opportunity, 2008. www.disabilityworks.org/downloads/disabilityworksDePaulStudyComprehensiveResults.pdf. Accessed 6/29/2012.

Hugenberg, Kurt, Galen V. Bodenhausen, and Melissa McLain. "Framing Discrimination: Effects of Inclusion Versus Exclusion Mind-Sets on Stereotypic Judgments." *Journal of Personality and Social Psychology* 91 (2006): 1020-1031.

Hunt, Courtney. "Social Screening: Candidates – and Employers – Beware." *Social Media in Organizations Community.* October 15, 2010. www.sminorgs.net/2010/10/social-screening-candidates-and-employers-beware.html. Accessed 6/29/2012.

June, Audrey Williams. "Faculty Job Interviews Move from Scholarly Meetings to Campuses." *Chronicle of Higher Education.* May 2, 2010. http://chronicle.com/article/Faculty-Job-Interviews-Move/65336. Accessed 2/16/2012.

Kutcher, Eugene J. and Jennifer DeNicolis Bragger. "Selection Interviews of Overweight Job Applicants: Can Structure Reduce the Bias?" *Journal of Applied Social Psychology* 34;10 (2004): 1993-2022.

Layne, Peggy. "Perspectives on Leadership from Female Engineering Deans." *Leadership and Management in Engineering* 10;4 (2010): 185-190.

Levin, Irwin P., Mary E. Huneke, and J.D. Jasper. "Information Processing at Successive Stages of Decision Making: Need for Cognition and Inclusion-Exclusion Effects." *Organizational Behavior and Human Decision Processes* 82;2 (2000): 171-193.

Liberman, Nira and Jens Förster. "Expression After Suppression: A Motivational Explanation of Postsuppressional Rebound." *Journal of Personality and Social Psychology* 79;2 (2000): 190-203.

Lowery, Brian S., Curtis D. Hardin, and Stacey Sinclair. "Social Influence Effects on Automatic Racial Prejudice." *Journal of Personality and Social Psychology* 81;5 (2001): 842-855.

Macrae, C. Neil, Galen V. Bodenhausen, Alan B. Milne, and Jolanda Jetten. "Out of Mind but Back in Sight: Stereotypes on the Rebound." *Journal of Personality and Social Psychology* 67;5 (1994): 808-817.

Martell, Richard F. "Sex Bias at Work: The Effects of Attentional and Memory Demands on Performance Ratings of Men and Women." *Journal of Applied Social Psychology* 21;23 (1991): 1939-1960.

McCain, Kathy. "Video Conferencing Etiquette." University of Wisconsin–Madison Department of Family Medicine. https://inside.fammed.wisc.edu/documents/3447. Accessed 1/18/2012.

Monteith, Margo J., Jeffrey W. Sherman, and Patricia G. Devine. "Suppression as a Stereotype Control Strategy." *Personality and Social Psychology Review* 2;1 (1998): 63-82.

Moody, JoAnn. *Rising Above Cognitive Errors: Guidelines for Search, Tenure Review, and Other Evaluation Committees.* JoAnn Moody, 2010. www.DiversityOnCampus.com. Accessed 9/10/2012.

Moss-Racusin, Corinne A., John F. Dovidio, Victoria L. Brescoll, Mark J. Graham, and Jo Handelsman. "Science Faculty's Subtle Gender Biases Favor Male Students." *Proceedings of the National Academy of Sciences (PNAS)* 109;41 (2012): 16474-16479.

National Science Foundation. "Survey of Earned Doctorates (SED) Tabulation Engine." https://ncses.norc.org/NSFTabEngine. Accessed 9/20/2012.

"Number of Full-Time Faculty Members by Sex, Rank, and Racial and Ethnic Group, 2007." Almanac of Higher Education, 2010. *Chronicle of Higher Education*, August 24, 2009. http://chronicle.com/article/Number-of-Full-Time-Faculty/47992. Accessed 9/10/2012.

Page, Scott E. *The Difference: How the Power of Diversity Creates Better Groups, Firms, Schools, and Societies.* Princeton, NJ: Princeton University Press, 2007.

Paludi, Michele A. and William D. Bauer. "Goldberg Revisited: What's in an Author's Name." *Sex Roles* 9;3 (1983): 387-390.

Phelan, Julie E., Corinne A. Moss-Racusin, and Laurie A. Rudman. "Competent Yet Out in the Cold: Shifting Criteria for Hiring Reflect Backlash Toward Agentic Women." *Psychology of Women Quarterly* 32;4 (2008): 406-413.

Pribbenow, Dean. "Improving the interview and selection process." Madison, WI: University of Wisconsin-Madison Office of Quality Improvement, 2002. http://go.wisc.edu/905o7d.

Project Implicit. Implicit Association Test (IAT). https://implicit.harvard.edu/implicit. Accessed 3/6/2012.

Raphael, Rebecca. "Academe is Silent about Deaf Professors." *Chronicle of Higher Education* 53;4 (2006): 56.

Reilly, Nora P., Shawn P. Bocketti, Stephen A. Maser, and Craig L. Wennet. "Benchmarks Affect Perceptions of Prior Disability in a Structured Interview." *Journal of Business and Psychology* 20;4 (2006): 489-500.

Ridgeway, Cecilia L. "Gender, Status, and Leadership." *Journal of Social Issues* 57;4 (2001): 637-655.

Rose, Sarah F. "Disability and the Academic Job Market." *Disability Studies Quarterly* 28;3 (2008). http://dsq-sds.org/article/view/111/111. Accessed 2/17/2012.

Rubini, Monica and Michela Menegatti. "Linguistic Bias in Personnel Selection." *Journal of Language and Social Psychology* 27;2 (2008): 168-181.

Schiebinger, Londa, Andrea Davies Henderson, and Shannon K. Gilmartin. *Dual-Career Academic Couples: What Universities Need to Know.* Stanford, CA: Michelle R. Clayman Institute for Gender Research, Stanford University, 2008.

Schmader, Toni, Jessica Whitehead, and Vicki H. Wysocki. "A Linguistic Comparison of Letters of Recommendation for Male and Female Chemistry and Biochemistry Job Applicants." *Sex Roles* 57;7/8 (2007): 509-514.

Smith, Daryl G. "How to Diversify the Faculty." *Academe* 86;5 (2000): 48-52.

Smith, Daryl G., Lisa E. Wolf, and Bonnie E. Busenberg. *Achieving Faculty Diversity: Debunking the Myths.* Washington, D.C.: Association of American Colleges and Universities, 1996.

Smith, Daryl G. et al. *Diversity Works: The Emerging Picture of How Students Benefit.* Washington, D.C.: Association of American Colleges and Universities, 1997.

Stangor, Charles and David McMillan. "Memory for Expectancy-Congruent and Expectancy-Incongruent Information: A Review of the Social and Social Developmental Literatures." *Psychological Bulletin* 111;1 (1992): 42-61.

Steele, Claude M. "A Threat in the Air: How Stereotypes Shape Intellectual Identity and Performance." *American Psychologist* 52;6 (1997): 613-629.

Steinpreis Rhea E., Katie A. Anders, and Dawn Ritzke. "The Impact of Gender on the Review of the Curricula Vitae of Job Applicants and Tenure Candidates: A National Empirical Study." *Sex Roles* 41;7/8 (1999): 509-528.

"Top 100 Producers of Minority Degrees, 2012." *Diverse Issues in Higher Education.* http://diverseeducation.com/top100. Accessed 9/28/2012.

Tosi, Henry L. and Steven W. Einbender. "The Effects of the Type and Amount of Information in Sex Discrimination Research: A Meta-Analysis." *Academy of Management Journal* 28;3 (1985): 712-723.

Trix, Frances and Carolyn Psenka. "Exploring the Color of Glass: Letters of Recommendation for Female and Male Medical Faculty." *Discourse & Society* 14;2 (2003): 191-220.

Turner, Caroline Sotello Viernes. *Diversifying the Faculty: A Guidebook for Search Committees.* Washington, D.C.: Association of American Colleges and Universities, 2002.

Uhlmann, Eric Luis and Geoffrey L. Cohen. "Constructed Criteria: Redefining Merit to Justify Discrimination." *Psychological Science* 16;6 (2005): 474-480.

Uhlmann, Eric Luis and Geoffrey L. Cohen. "'I Think it, therefore it's True': Effects of Self-Perceived Objectivity on Hiring Discrimination." *Organizational Behavior and Human Decision Processes* 104;2 (2007): 207-223.

United States Department of Education. "Lists of Postsecondary Institutions Enrolling Populations with Significant Percentages of Minority Students." http://www2.ed.gov/about/offices/list/ocr/edlite-minorityinst-list.html. Accessed 6/29/2012.

United States Department of Labor. "Hiring: Affirmative Action." http://www.dol.gov/dol/topic/hiring/affirmativeact.htm. Accessed 3/28/2012.

United States Equal Employment Opportunity Commission (EEOC). www.eeoc.gov/eeoc. Accessed 3/28/2012.

University of Michigan ADVANCE. "Candidate EvaluationTool." www.umich.edu/%7Eadvproj/CandidateEvaluationTool.doc. Accessed 7/18/2012.

University of Michigan ADVANCE. *Handbook for Faculty Searches and Hiring, Academic Year 2009-10.* Ann Arbor: University of Michigan ADVANCE, 2009. www.advance.rackham.umich.edu/handbook.pdf. Accessed 7/18/2012.

University of Wisconsin-Madison, Office of Academic Planning and Analysis. "Summary of Faculty Recruitment Efforts." 2010-11.

University of Wisconsin-Madison, Office of Human Resources. "Appropriate and Inappropriate Interview Questions." http://go.wisc.edu/54sqgx. Accessed 9/28/2012.

University of Wisconsin-Madison, Office of Human Resources. "OHR Recruitment Toolkit." https://recruitment.wisc.edu. Accessed 9/12/2012.

University of Wisconsin-Madison, Office of Quality Improvement and Office of Human Resource Development. "Academic Leadership Support: Confidentiality." http://go.wisc.edu/3idbel. Accessed 9/11/2012.

University of Wisconsin-Madison, Office of Quality Improvement. "How to Lead Effective Meetings." http://quality.wisc.edu/effective-meetings.htm. Accessed 9/11/2012.

van Ommeren, Jos, Reinout E. de Vries, Giovanni Russo, and Mark van Ommeren. "Context in Selection of Men and Women in Hiring Decisions: Gender Composition of the Applicant Pool." *Psychological Reports* 96;2 (2005): 349-360.

Wennerås, Christine and Agnes Wold. "Nepotism and Sexism in Peer-Review." *Nature* 387;6631 (1997): 341-343.

Whatley, Mariamne. "Writing a Position Vacancy Listing (PVL) for a Faculty or Nationally Recruited Academic Staff Search." http://go.wisc.edu/2f4yp1. (Document removed from site.)

Wigboldus, Daniël H. J., Gün R. Semin, and Russell Spears. "How do we Communicate Stereotypes? Linguistic Bases and Inferential Consequences." *Journal of Personality and Social Psychology* 78;1 (2000): 5-18.

Wilkinson, Sophie L. "Approaching a Workplace for All: Chemists with Disabilities Profit from a Mix of Pragmatism and Assertiveness on the Job." *Chemical & Engineering News* 79;46 (2001): 55-59.

Wyer, Natalie A., Jeffrey W. Sherman, and Steven J. Stroessner. "The Roles of Motivation and Ability in Controlling the Consequences of Stereotype Suppression." *Personality and Social Psychology Bulletin* 26;1 (2000): 13-25.

Yaniv, Ilan and Yaacov Schul. "Acceptance and Elimination Procedures in Choice: Noncomplementarity and the Role of Implied Status Quo." *Organizational Behavior and Human Decision Processes* 82;2 (2000): 293-313.

The Young Philosopher. "End Conference Interviews." *Inside Higher Ed.* February 11, 2011. www.insidehighered.com/advice/2011/02/11/a_call_to_end_conference_interviews. Accessed 2/16/2012.

CPSIA information can be obtained
at www.ICGtesting.com
Printed in the USA
FFOW02n1627070216
21226FF